YORK NOTES

General Editors: Professor A.N. Jⴰᵤₐ.
of Stirling) & Professor Suheil Bushrui (*American University of Beirut*)

John Milton

PARADISE LOST
BOOKS IV & IX

Notes by Richard James Beck

OBE MA (OXFORD) PH D (ST ANDREWS)
Former Professor, University of Malta

LONGMAN
YORK PRESS

YORK PRESS
Immeuble Esseily, Place Riad Solh, Beirut.

LONGMAN GROUP LIMITED
London
Associated companies, branches and representatives
throughout the world

© Librairie du Liban 1980

First published 1980
ISBN 0 582 78219 8
Printed in Hong Kong by
Wing Tai Cheung Printing Co Ltd

Contents

Part 1

Introduction

Milton's times

The world into which John Milton was born in 1608 was a troubled and confused one; and, until his death in 1674, Milton lived through a period of turmoil and violent change. By 1608 King James I had been on the throne of England for five years; coming south from Scotland after the death of Elizabeth I, he lacked the popularity of his doughty predecessor, on both national and personal grounds. Also, he was extravagant in an age when the royal revenues were steadily decreasing in value; and, believing that he had been called to rule by God's command rather than by the will of the people or the consent of their representatives, James clashed frequently and violently with Parliament over the control of the country's government, and particularly its finances. An early struggle for control of the judges was resolved in favour of Parliament by 1621. King James also thought that he should control the Church through its bishops; but a group of men, increasing in numbers and strength as the years went by, believed that the English Reformation, begun by Henry VIII with the double purpose of divorcing a queen who could not give him a male heir and of stripping the many rich monasteries and abbeys of their treasures, scarcely justified its name. Realising that such abuses as one priest holding more than one living were being retained, and that the authority of the Pope had been replaced by that of the King as head of the English Church, these men, the Puritans, as their name implies, strove for a purer, more austere form of worship and Church organisation. Puritanism is not a religion, nor confined to any one sect: it is an attitude of mind. These two forces of Puritanism and Parliamentarianism together resisted royal absolutism, at first by constitutional means, seeking to make the granting of revenue dependent upon the reform of abuses; and, from 1642 onwards, by force of arms.

James I's son and successor, Charles I, quarrelled bitterly with his Parliaments from his accession in 1625 until 1629, when he determined to rule without a parliament at all; this period was called the Personal Rule. Forced by a Scottish invasion to recall Parliament in 1640 to vote funds for an army, Charles disagreed with them all over again, saw his chief minister, Strafford, and his Archbishop of Canterbury, Laud, removed from authority and executed, and, finally, in 1642, took up arms to crush the forces of Parliament. Successful in the early stages of the war, Charles faced a powerful combination in the alliance of Parliament with the Scottish Covenanters, the loyalty of London to the Parliamentary cause, and the brilliant generalship of Oliver Cromwell. Charles's fortunes declined, he was beaten in decisive battles at Marston Moor in 1644 and Naseby in 1645, surrendered, was imprisoned, tried, condemned and beheaded in 1649.

Thereafter Cromwell ruled England as Lord Protector until his death in 1658; but the Commonwealth had become increasingly unpopular, and there was no strong character to succeed Cromwell; so in 1660 the royal house of Stuart was restored to the English throne in the person of Charles II, morally profligate but politically astute. He had been on the throne for fourteen years when Milton died in 1674, and a further fourteen years were to pass before a second revolution continued the process of securing parliamentary rule in England and making its monarchy more constitutional.

Milton's life

No other English poet has been so closely involved in the events of his time as Milton; and only Wordsworth has ever told us so much about himself. In Milton's case there were two reasons for this. Much of his work as Latin Secretary to Cromwell consisted of writing pamphlets justifying Government policy, and these pamphlets and the ones inspired by the exiled Royalists did not hesitate to stoop to the most scurrilous personal details – and Milton sought to counteract these attacks on himself by producing autobiographical evidence. The second reason is that Milton felt from an early age that he was destined 'to leave something so written to after-times as they should not willingly let it die', and therefore believed that posterity would wish to know as much as possible about him. In his pamphlet *The Second Defence of the People of England*, which is in large part a defence of himself, Milton tells us,

> My father destined me from a child to the pursuits of literature; and my appetite for knowledge was so voracious, that, from twelve years of age, I hardly ever left my studies, or went to bed before midnight. This primarily led to my loss of sight. My eyes were naturally weak, and I was subject to frequent head-aches; which, however, could not chill the ardour of my curiosity, or retard the progress of my improvement. My father had me daily instructed in the grammar-school, and by other masters at home. He then, after I had acquired a proficiency in various languages, and had made a considerable progress in philosophy, sent me to the University of Cambridge. Here I passed seven years in the usual course of instruction and study, with

the approbation of the good, and without any stain upon my character, till I took the degree of Master of Arts. After this I did not, as this miscreant feigns, run away into Italy, but of my own accord retired to my father's house, whither I was accompanied by the regrets of most of the fellows of the college, who shewed me no common marks of friendship and esteem. On my father's estate, where he had determined to pass the remainder of his days, I enjoyed an interval of uninterrupted leisure, which I entirely devoted to the perusal of the Greek and Latin classics; though I occasionally visited the metropolis, either for the sake of purchasing books, or of learning something new in mathematics or in music, in which I, at that time, found a source of pleasure and amusement. In this manner I spent five years till my mother's death. (*Milton's Prose Works*, ed. Bohn, London, 1848, Vol. I, pp. 254–5; hereafter referred to as 'Bohn')

There is much of interest in this passage: the reference to Milton's weak eyes – the poet who wrote *Paradise Lost* was at the time of writing it totally blind, claiming that he had sacrificed his eyes in the service of liberty and Cromwell's government; affection for and gratitude to his father, which reveals a gentler side of an otherwise unloving nature (his only real friend, Charles Diodati, died young, and the famous elegy on Lycidas was in fact a poem more concerned with Milton than with his Cambridge contemporary, Edward King); and the years of dedication to private study, financed by his father, which resulted in *Paradise Lost's* being a poem difficult for the modern reader to understand by reason of its extensive learning and wealth of allusion.

After Cambridge and Horton (the estate in Buckinghamshire referred to in the quotation), Milton began a European tour. He visited Galileo in Fiesole, near Florence; Galileo is the only one of Milton's contemporaries to merit a mention in *Paradise Lost* (he is named in V, 260 and is the 'Tuscan artist' of I, 288). Milton cut short his tour because of the situation in England, but did not hurry unduly on his way home, and did not join the armies of the Parliament on his return, devoting himself instead to the education of his two nephews, the Phillips brothers. Indeed, when Prince Rupert's cavaliers reached the outskirts of London late in 1642, Milton wrote and displayed on his door the sonnet *Captain or colonel or knight in arms*, not very courageously begging that his house might be spared as was the poet Pindar's when Alexander the Great captured Thebes in 355BC. In the event, the cavaliers were beaten back.

The years 1642–3 mark the end of what might be called Milton's first period, and the beginning of his second. From a personal point of view, his prolonged education was complete. Poetically, he had already written his early lyric poems: the *Nativity Ode*; the companion poems

L'Allegro (the happy man) and *Il Penseroso* (the serious man); the masque, *Comus*; the pastoral elegy, *Lycidas*; and a number of sonnets, among them the autobiographical Twenty-Third Birthday sonnet. Milton's second period was one of public office and political pamphleteering, with a few sonnets the only poetry. Then, with his blindness, came the third period of personal defeat and disillusion, but poetically the great days of his three long poems, *Paradise Lost, Paradise Regained* and *Samson Agonistes.*

To return to the beginning of Milton's second period: in 1642 or 1643, Milton married Mary Powell, the daughter of a Royalist house with which his father had had business dealings; indeed, despite Mary's obvious physical attraction for Milton, this was primarily a marriage by arrangement, and was certainly no love match on her side. Mary speedily found the Puritan austerity and intellectual stature of her new husband too much for her, and promptly returned home. The war made reclamation difficult. This marriage is important because of the events it set in train. Had it not been for his own bitter personal experience, Milton would not have sought so vehemently to justify divorce by reference to scripture in four pamphlets. These pamphlets were condemned by theologians in Milton's own party, which was already, in 1643, severely limiting the licensing of books. Believing that two of his most strongly held principles were endangered – the right of individual interpretation of scripture and freedom of speech and writing – Milton in 1644 published *Areopagitica,* his noblest pamphlet, inspired by his love of liberty and free of the usual personal scurrility. His sympathies were now with the Cromwellian and army section of the Parliament side, with its greater religious tolerance, rather than with the austere Presbyterians who insisted on the doctrine of predestination and its consequent limitation of individual freedom. In 1649 Milton was made Latin Secretary to the Commonwealth with the official title of 'Secretary for the Foreign Tongues'; the revolutionary government used Latin as its language of diplomacy, and the learned Milton was a natural choice. His main tasks were to write pamphlets justifying Government policy, particularly the execution of the King; to defeat the champions of the Royalist cause on paper; and to compose official despatches to the courts of Europe, from Stockholm to Savoy, for the victories of the English New Model Army he had created had made Cromwell a man to be reckoned with in international relations.

By 1652 Milton had lost his sight completely, and in 1655 he was allowed a substitute Secretary. He now turned his mind back to poetry, though he continued to write anti-monarchical pamphlets until 1660, the year of the Restoration. Milton's third period, that of his long poems, coincides approximately with the first fourteen years of the Restoration (1660–74), though there are grounds for believing that he wrote Satan's address to the sun *(Paradise Lost*, IV, 32–113) as early as 1642. At the time of the Restoration, Milton as a well-known Cromwellian was in some physical danger, but the Royalist poet Davenant, placing poetry before politics, concealed him until the risk was past. Henceforward Milton, blind, ailing and impoverished, lived quietly and unpersecuted in the midst of his triumphant enemies until his death in 1674, visited by many friends and admirers.

Milton's relationships with his family are significant, and his view of the status of women affects *Paradise Lost* profoundly in the books where Eve appears. The relative status of man and wife is a theme of recurring interest in Books IV and IX, as Part 3, Commentary, in these notes makes clear. Relationships among the men in Milton's family were good; he loved his father deeply, and took him in and cared for him in his old age, addressing the poem 'Ad Patrem' to him; his nephews, the two brothers Phillips, continued to visit him after the Restoration, acted at times as his amanuenses (so necessary for a blind poet), and each wrote a memoir of him after his death. But he did not inspire love in women. His first wife left him soon after they were married, and was only reconciled to him when the Royalist cause was already lost; his three daughters were all her children. Four years after she died in childbirth, he married again, in 1656, only to lose his second wife in the same way; it is generally accepted that the sonnet 'Methought I saw my late espoused Saint' is dedicated to her, despite recent critical assertions that the only wife Milton ever 'saw' was his first. In his third period (he took one wife in each), Milton married for a third time; it is difficult to avoid concluding that his main reason was to ease the housekeeping problems of a blind man. His daughters were made to read to him in languages they did not understand, and only the youngest, Deborah, spoke kindly of him after his death, and that when his reputation as a great poet was already established; the children, on their side, sought to cheat him out of the marketing money and to sell his books. And yet Milton did not despise women. He thought the male partner should be predominant, but a woman like Eve has grace and dignity to match Adam's male strength and intellect, and true wedded bliss such as we find in *Paradise Lost*, IV, comes from the perfect union of two different natures.

This divergence between precept and practice in his attitude to women is only one of the contradictions in Milton that make him so difficult to understand. A fervent lover of liberty and individual freedom, he for some time allied himself with Presbyterians who condemned free will; and he certainly did not believe in the basic equality of all men, regarding himself as set apart and destined for greatness, the chosen prophet of the new dispensation under which God intended Cromwellian England to teach the rest of Europe how to live. And his picture of Satan as the grand rebel against imposed authority, divine and benevolent though that authority may be, has caused the poets William Blake (1757–1827) and P. B. Shelley (1792–1822), to name but two, to maintain that Milton was of the Devil's party without knowing it.

Milton's cosmology

One further contradiction demands fuller treatment: Milton's mixture of the two cosmologies, the Ptolemaic and the Copernican, in *Paradise Lost*. More far-reaching than the purely national quarrels between the King on the one hand and Parliament and the Puritans on the other, the changeover from the Ptolemaic to the Copernican system of cosmology affected the whole Western world; the poet John Donne (1571 or 1572–1631) wrote with truth in the *First Anniversary*, 'And new Philosophy calls all in doubt'.

Throughout the Middle Ages it had been accepted that man was the centre of the universe and his Earth the hub of a rotating planetary system. The seven known planets orbited the Earth, each one's atmosphere pushing round the one next inside it by friction, thus creating a note of music; all the notes together made up the heavenly harmony, or music of the spheres. The outermost orbit, that of the planet Saturn, was itself surrounded by the sphere of the fixed stars (*Paradise Lost*, III, 481) and outside that again was the vast expanse of the waters of the firmament, also called by Milton the Crystalline Sphere, or the Hyaline (*Paradise Lost*, VII, 619). These waters of the firmament, as distinct from the waters on the earth and under the earth, had been used by God as an insulating jacket designed to protect His newly created universe from the excesses of cold and heat in the region of Chaos through which Satan flies at the end of Book II. The whole universe was suspended from Heaven (also frequently called the Empyrean) by a golden chain. In the area outside the Hyaline was the sphere of the Primum Mobile, or First Mover. This Primum Mobile transformed the love of God for mankind into energy and provided the impetus that made the whole universe rotate; the Middle Ages believed literally that it was Divine Love that made the world go round.

In Heaven, God sits on His throne supported by four seraphim, the most powerful of the nine orders of angels which had remained loyal. The rebel tenth who had revolted under Satan had been hurled down into another dread realm, Hell, created for them to occupy beyond the domain of Chaos and Old Night. In the second half of Book II of *Paradise Lost*, Satan breaks out of his prison in Hell and wins his way through the abyss ruled by Chaos and Old Night to the outer surface of our universe. Deceiving Uriel, regent of the sun, he flies down to Eden. The subsequent movements of both Satan and the guardians of Paradise are explained in Books IV and IX with detailed astronomical references.

Some of the features of this cosmology have been added to the Ptolemaic system as amended by Alfonso X of Castile in the thirteenth century; the golden chain on which the universe hangs, and the site and physical features of Hell, for example. But the most interesting point about Milton's cosmology is this: why, when he knew of the discoveries Galileo had made with his telescope – as Book VIII clearly proves – and must have accepted the validity of the Copernican cosmology, which recognises that the Sun and not the Earth is the centre around which our planetary system revolves, did Milton base his universe upon the Ptolemaic pattern? The answer lies in the literary advantages of accepting the older though erroneous concept: it was known, and Copernicanism was strongly resisted and only slowly accepted; the Ptolemaic system was orderly, it laid down limits within which Milton found it easier to work, and it made God and man the two ends of a chain – man can ascend, onward and ever upward, to union with the divinity, and this could never have happened in an open-ended Copernican universe.

Cosmology is not of major concern in Books IV and IX; but see the notes to IX, 52 and particularly IV, 592–5, where one of the main differences between the Ptolemaic and Copernican systems is considered.

The epic

Paradise Lost is the only modern English representative of the epic genre; we exclude the so-called 'brief epic' represented by *Paradise Regained*. Epic itself is a very ancient form of poetry, originating in an age before writing, when long narratives dealing with the mighty deeds of the military aristocracy were recited to an assembled company, on long winter evenings or after a feasting. The narrative consisted of a series of loosely linked and easily detachable episodes, to enable the overall length to be varied as circumstances demanded, and centred on the exploits of some national hero who was something more than human if slightly less than divine, probably with one divine parent who helped him, argued his case in celestial councils, and endowed him with extraordinary qualities. To provide some rest for the reciter and some relief for the listeners, stock passages came to be included in the epic: the hero's ancestry; the description and history of his weapons; a council or debate, usually in heaven; and so on. These epics are called Primary Epics because their characteristics naturally reflect the society that gave them birth; and the most famous examples are the *Iliad* and the *Odyssey*, supposedly by the blind poet Homer, whose authorship and even whose existence are uncertain.

The main interest for readers of *Paradise Lost* lies in the Secondary Epic of the Latin poet Virgil (70–19BC). His great work, the *Aeneid*, was intended to be read by an individual in solitude, not recited to an assembly of listeners. The grandeur which had been natural to Primary Epic was artificially reproduced in Virgil by means of the conscious literary style of an individual artist, while the genealogies of weapons, long similes containing complete pictures in words, celestial councils and debates were imitated in a serious and lofty tone. Most remarkably, the character of the epic hero was altered to suit the changing spirit of the age. No longer is Achilles, seeking glory on the field of battle, the ideal; the Homeric-type hero in the *Aeneid*, Turnus, is defeated by a new ideal, Aeneas, still a hero with one divine and one mortal parent, still a brave and skilful fighter when the need arises, but also a more philosophical hero who must learn to control himself before he is judged fit to found an empire. These two elements, the consciously created grand style and the hero who reflects the spirit of a new and more sophisticated age, were vital to Milton, as they must also be to any student of *Paradise Lost*.

The end of the fifteenth century saw the rise of another type of epic, the Romantic Epic of the Italian poets Ariosto (1474–1533) and Boiardo (1441?–94), characterised by exaggeration and, as its name implies, no claim to historical truth. More significant were the Renaissance epics, in which the poets sought to do for their own countries what Virgil had done for Imperial Rome, and for their vernacular languages what Virgil had done for Latin. *Os Lusíadas*, by the Portuguese poet Luis de Camoëns (*c.*1524–80), published in 1572, is the best example of this type; it sings the praises of Vasco da Gama, the great Portuguese navigator, and actually begins with the same words as the *Aeneid*, 'Of arms and the man I sing'. Also of importance is the *Gerusalemme Liberata* by the Italian poet Torquato Tasso (1544–95), which deals with the liberation of Jerusalem in the Second Crusade – a religious subject of more than purely national interest; in this it resembles *Paradise Lost*.

The epic elements in *Paradise Lost*, Books IV and IX, will be noted in the Commentary, and the grandeur of Milton's style and the characteristics of the Miltonic hero discussed. But here it is convenient to stress how Milton fits into the developing epic tradition. Determined to write some great work, he pondered over three problems: what literary form his great work should take; who was most suited to be its hero; and in what language it should be written. In the *Reason of Church Government* (1641), Milton lays his options clearly before us:

> Time serves not now, and perhaps I might seem too profuse to give any certain account of what the mind at home, in the spacious circuits of her musing, hath liberty to propose to herself, though of highest hope and hardest attempting; whether that epic form whereof the two poems of Homer, and those other two of Virgil and Tasso, are a

diffuse, and the book of Job a brief model: of whether the rules of Aristotle herein are strictly to be kept, or nature to be followed, which in them that know art, and use judgment, is no transgression, but an enriching of art: and lastly, what king or knight, before the conquest, might be chosen in whom to lay the pattern of a Christian hero. And as Tasso gave to a prince of Italy his choice whether he would command him to write of Godfrey's expedition against the Infidels, or Belisarius against the Goths, or Charlemain against the Lombards; if to the instinct of nature and the emboldening of art aught may be trusted, and that there be nothing adverse in our climate, or the fate of this age, it haply would be no rashness, from an equal diligence and inclination, to present the like offer in our own ancient stories; or whether those dramatic constitutions, wherein Sophocles and Euripides reign, shall be found more doctrinal and exemplary to a nation. The scripture also affords us a divine pastoral drama in the Song of Solomon, consisting of two persons, and a double chorus, as Origen rightly judges. And the Apocalypse of St John is the majestic image of a high and stately tragedy, shutting up and intermingling her solemn scenes and acts with a sevenfold chorus of hallelujahs and harping symphonies: and this my opinion the grave authority of Pareus, commenting that book, is sufficient to confirm. Or if occasion shall lead, to imitate those magnific odes and hymns, wherein Pindarus and Callimachus are in most things worthy, some others in their frame judicious, in their matter most an end faulty. But those frequent songs throughout the law and prophets beyond all these, not in their divine argument alone, but in the very critical art of composition, may be easily made appear over all the kinds of lyric poesy to be incomparable. (Bohn, II. 478–79)

Long epic, short epic, drama, pastoral and lyric are all here considered as possible forms, foreshadowing not merely *Paradise Lost* but *Paradise Regained* and *Samson Agonistes*; also 'the pattern of a Christian hero'. Milton's preference for scriptural literature over the classical, not only in subject but in style, may seem strange, but it is difficult to contradict him when he knew both languages and both literatures thoroughly and we do not. Eventually, Milton rejected the choice of a national hero, King Arthur, and a national subject, in favour of the universal subject of the Fall of Man. He chose the form of the long epic and, rejecting the general view that English was a shifting sand while Latin was lasting marble, decided, like a true Renaissance poet, to do for English what Virgil had done for Latin. 'I applied myself,' he wrote (Bohn, II, 478), 'to that resolution, which Ariosto followed against the persuasions of Bembo, to fix all the industry and art I could unite to the adorning of my native tongue.'

A note on the text

Every year in the decade beginning in 1652 has been put forward as the date when *Paradise Lost* was begun (though some lines of Book IV were probably written ten years earlier). All that is known for certain is that it was first published in 1667; but the assurance of the Quaker Thomas Ellwood, who found Milton a cottage in the country during the Great Plague, that Milton gave him the manuscript to read at that time, may be accepted as evidence that the poem was complete by 1665. There was a second edition in 1674; Milton then divided the original Books VII and X into two each, thus making up the customary epic number of twelve. *Paradise Lost* continued to be admired and its elevated language imitated throughout the eighteenth century, and it did not lapse into oblivion with the Romantic Revival, for the poet Wordsworth (1770–1850) was one of Milton's greatest admirers. During the Victorian period *Paradise Lost* was one of the few books accepted as being suitable for Sunday reading, and the twentieth century has seen the publication of many editions. The Oxford Milton (1904; revised 1969) contains the complete poems, without commentary or notes, but with the earliest possible spelling and punctuation, to which the blind and therefore sound-sensitive Milton paid such careful attention. The Milton volume in the Longmans Annotated English Poets series, edited by A. Fowler and J. Carey, Longman, London, 1968, has a modernised text and is fully and eruditely annotated. A. W. Verity's volume of notes to his own edition of *Paradise Lost*, Cambridge University Press, Cambridge, 1936, is still a valuable work of reference, and numerous paperback editions of two or more books of *Paradise Lost*, annotated and with critical introduction, have appeared since the end of the Second World War, designed to provide the necessary basic background for a study of Milton's text at a reasonable price.

Part 2

Summaries
of PARADISE LOST

A general summary

When the second edition of *Paradise Lost* was published in 1674, Milton added the *Arguments* which precede each book; these summarise the contents in the author's own words. The whole work is not one continuous narrative; in true Virgilian epic tradition, the story begins in the middle, and earlier events are presented to the reader by various means – dreams, reminiscences, and conversations. Milton first states his general purpose, to tell the story of man's fall; but we do not learn of the events leading up to this fall, and the consequences which stem from it, until much later. In Books V and VI, the seraph Raphael, sent down to Paradise by God to enlighten and warn Adam, tells him of the revolt of Satan against God and how, inspired by pride, ambition and envy, he seduced one-tenth of the angelic host into following him. Summarily defeated by God's Son in a terrible war in Heaven, Satan and his followers are hurled down to the place of fiery torment prepared for them, Hell. Continuing his story in Book VII, Raphael tells Adam how the universe was created, culminating in the creation of man himself. Adam, having in Book VIII asked some questions on astronomy which reveal Milton's knowledge of Galileo's discoveries, proceeds to give his own version of his creation and that of Eve. With a final admonition on the value of Temperance, or self-control, Raphael departs. This means that the first acts of the drama actually take place in Books V–VIII.

After the initial statement of general purpose, Book I takes up the story of the rebel angels, newly arrived in Hell, into which they have been hurled following their defeat in the war in Heaven. Their situation, individual characters and occupations are described, and in Book II they meet in council to decide what is to be done. Finally, it is agreed that Satan shall fly off to the new world of man to see if he can strike at God through His new creation. Satan's escape from Hell, his meeting with Sin and Death and his perilous passage to the surface of our world are then described.

In Book III the scene switches to Heaven, where God delivers a long homily on man's freedom to choose between good and evil; complicated philosophical considerations of free will and predestination (Book III) and the doctrine of temperance (Book IX) are all vitally necessary for a full understanding of Milton. At the end of God's speech foreshadowing man's freely chosen disobedience and fall, the Son offers himself as the ransom for mankind and God accepts his sacrifice. Satan meanwhile has landed on the rim of the universe, and, finding his way in, flies down to the Sun and thence to Earth. In Book IV he observes the marital happiness of Adam and Eve and is aroused to a fury of envy. Uriel, regent of the Sun, who has directed Satan on his way, observes his behaviour and reports it to Gabriel, commander of the angelic patrol in Eden. Satan is thus frustrated in his first attempt to tempt Eve by means of a dream and is expelled from Paradise. God then sends Raphael, as we have seen, to alert Adam to the situation and to warn him. The warning is in vain, as God had foreknown it would be, and in Book IX Milton changes his tone to tragic, claiming nevertheless that his theme is more truly heroic than the stories of Classical and Romantic epic. Satan succeeds in his design of persuading Eve to taste the forbidden fruit, and Adam also eats, determined to share Eve's fate, 'not deceived, but fondly overcome by female charm'. They become intemperate, first through lust and then through anger, blaming each other bitterly. Book X is a book of retribution and reconciliation. The Son comes down to Eden to pronounce God's sentence of expulsion, toil and mortality, tempered by the promise of ultimate victory over evil. Adam and Eve are reconciled and accept their fate with resignation. Satan meanwhile has not gone unpunished. Returning to Hell in triumph, instead of the expected acclamation he is greeted by a universal hiss; for all his followers have become serpents, and he himself is forthwith transformed into the greatest serpent of them all.

The two concluding books of *Paradise Lost*, originally one, conform to another epic tradition, that of looking into the future; as Aeneas was permitted to foresee the Empire of Augustus (27BC–AD14), so Adam is shown a synopsis of Jewish history down to the redemption of mankind by Christ on the Cross. The first part, to the Flood, he is shown by the Archangel Michael in a vision (Book XI), but Michael relates the second part of the story (Book XII) to spare Adam's sight. Reconciled to his fate by the promise of ultimate redemption coming after so much evil, Adam takes Eve by the hand and they pass out of Paradise to face the hardships of the outside world together.

Detailed summaries

Book IV, lines 1–31

As Satan approaches Eden, he hesitates while Milton bemoans the lack of a warning voice to apprise Adam and Eve of their approaching danger.

NOTES AND GLOSSARY:

lines 1–12:   These opening lines are full of verbal echoes of the Bible, Revelation 12:7–12:

'And there was war in heaven: Michael and his angels fought against the dragon . . . And the great dragon was cast out, that old serpent, called the Devil, and Satan . . . And I heard a loud voice saying in heaven . . . the accuser of our brethren is cast down . . . Therefore rejoice, ye heavens, and ye that dwell in them. Woe to the inhabiters of the earth and of the sea! for the devil is come down unto you, having great wrath, because he knoweth that he hath but a short time'.

Many of the nouns are chosen with their Greek etymology in mind: 'apocalypse', revelation, uncovering; 'dragon', serpent, that is, Satan; 'devil', slanderer, accuser.

the second rout: the one seen by St John in his vision; the first was the one related in *Paradise Lost*, VI, where Satan was expelled from Heaven following his unsuccessful rebellion

while time was: while there was still time

mortal snare: fatal trap

wreak: avenge

not rejoicing in his speed: Satan, so courageous before the event, hesitates now that the time for decisive action is at hand

nigh the birth: on the verge of realisation

rolling: moving onwards, usually of time

devilish engine: like the cannon used in the war in Heaven (VI, 484) Milton insists that hell is not merely external; Satan carries his own hell within him. See line 75

what must be worse: how he must become worse

meridian tower: the Sun crosses the meridian at midday, astrologically a suitable time for judicial consideration and decision

much revolving: pondering many things

Book IV, lines 32–113

Satan's address to the Sun resembles a dramatic soliloquy in which remorse is opposed to his will to resist, which finally triumphs.

NOTES AND GLOSSARY:

lines 32–41:	Milton's nephew, Edward Phillips, records that this speech was written as early as 1642; it is thus the earliest section of *Paradise Lost*. Since Milton was at that time considering writing a tragedy rather than an epic, the dramatic character of the speech is scarcely surprising
lines 33–5:	The Sun as a power occupies the planet of the same name, his 'solar dominion'. The brightness of the stars cannot approach its brilliance
add thy name:	This does not mean that Satan adds the Sun's name to something else, but that he actually names the Sun. To do this is bad magic: see Grimm's fairy-tale of Rumpelstiltzkin; even God refuses to reveal His name in Exodus 3:13–15
lines 42–7:	Satan recognises God's benevolence. He even admits what he elsewhere denies, that God created him and placed him in an exalted position
upbraided:	reproached, rebuked
sdeigned:	Milton improves the scansion by adopting the Italian form *sdegnare*, disdain
quit:	repay
still:	always
lines 55–7:	To be grateful in itself discharges the debt; but even when a debt has been repaid, a grateful sense of obligation remains
mean:	unimportant
Me miserable!:	a dramatic exclamation based on the Latin *me miserum*
lines 79–86:	Satan dismisses all thought of repentance because it would involve unconditional surrender to God, and he is too proud to do this or to betray the trust of those who followed him into rebellion. From this moment, Satan's determination to attack God through man never wavers
abide:	suffer on account of
high advanced:	raised up on high; refers to 'me' in line 89
by act of grace:	Satan maintains he should regain his former eminence by right and not by God's favour

line 95:	Milton favours the form 'highth', from Old English *híehtho*
violent and void:	null because made under duress. Satan rightly believes that an enforced submission to God would be neither genuine nor reliable
lines 108–13:	These lines contain the key to Satan's character in *Paradise Lost*; see Commentary, pp. 55–8, for detailed discussion
divided:	shared
more than half:	God rules Heaven, Satan hell. If he can win Earth, Satan will rule more than half the whole
raign:	reign, rule

Book IV, lines 114–30

Satan's inner struggle has been reflected in his face, and the archangel Uriel, the sharp-eyed regent of the Sun, who had directed Satan disguised as a young cherub to Earth at the end of the Book III, perceives that something is wrong and raises the alarm.

NOTES AND GLOSSARY:

Thrice changed with pale:	Satan was disguised as a young cherub (III, 636), and as such should have had a red face ('his borrowed visage') for the characteristic of the Cherubim was love; and love in medieval art was symbolically represented as being red. Thus, when Satan three times turns pale, he betrays himself as 'counterfeit'
distempers:	disturbances which upset the balance of the four humours (Blood, Phlegm, Choler and Melancholy) of which the human body was believed to be compounded, and which neutralised one another in a healthy person
perturbation:	sign of emotional disturbance
Artificer:	first creator
couched with:	united with in hiding
Assyrian mount:	Niphates, on the borders of Assyria and Armenia. See III, 742
disfigured:	Milton is very precise in his use of words: it was Satan's face (French *figure*) that betrayed him. It was generally believed that spirits could change their shapes but, nevertheless, could not disguise their natures

Book IV, lines 131–287

Satan now approaches and finally enters the Garden of Eden, which Milton describes at length. His description is based on the second chapter of Genesis, and is enriched by classical allusions.

NOTES AND GLOSSARY:

Paradise:	the actual garden situated in the land of Eden. The word has come through the Greek from a Persian original, meaning 'park'
champaign head:	open summit, unencumbered by trees. Milton, on Old Testament authority, imagines Paradise to be a garden situated on the summit of a wooded hill in the eastern part of the land of Eden. It is protected by a circular grassy mound, like a natural wall, inside which grow fruit trees, the tops of which can be seen from outside
hairy sides:	the tree-covered slopes of the hill on the summit of which the Garden is situated
grotesque:	intricately interwoven and picturesque
sylvan:	woodland
ranks:	the trees on the outer slopes ascended in tiers, like an amphitheatre
verdurous:	green and mossy
general sire:	Adam, father of us all
prospect large:	extensive view, panoramic vista
nether empire:	the land of Eden spreading outwards and downwards from the plateau of Paradise
enamelled:	fresh and varied, but with none of the modern connotation of hardness
humid bow:	rainbow. The Sun's beams made Eden more beautiful than the rainbow or the clouds of sunset
of:	following on
gentle gales:	breezes
Native perfumes:	scents belonging naturally to the plants concerned
Cape of Hope:	Cape of Good Hope, at the southern tip of Africa
Mozambic:	Mozambique, on the eastern coast of Africa. The trade route lay between Mozambique and the island of Madagascar
Sabean:	from Saba, or Sheba, now the Yemen. The smell of spices from *Arabia felix* wafted out to sea
line 164:	Ships beating up the coast of Africa would have to 'slack their course' when meeting a north-easterly trade wind from Arabia

bane:	destroyer
lines 168–71:	Tobias, son of Tobit, was sent into the land of Media by his father. Advised by the archangel Raphael in disguise, Tobias married Sara, daughter of Raguel, whose seven previous husbands had been killed off in succession by the jealous spirit Asmodeus; but Raphael instructed Tobias to burn the heart and liver of a fish, and the resultant stink was too much for Asmodeus, who fled into Egypt, where the angel bound him (see the Apocrypha, Book of Tobit, 6–8)
with a vengeance:	with all speed
savage:	wild
brake:	thicket
had perplexed:	would have perplexed
bound . . . bound:	a not very felicitous play upon words
lines 183–91:	Epic similes
cotes:	pens
secure:	over-confident (Latin *securus*)
lines 192–3:	These two lines establish beyond doubt Milton's conscious use of sound-values. The first line is full of round vowels and lengthening consonant-combinations; 'clomb' is made into a strong past definite to fit the pattern. In contrast to the grandeur of Satan's infiltration into Paradise, the despicable pettiness of the priests who violate God's church is accentuated by the thin vowels and sibilants of the second line
lewd:	ignorant, vile
line 195:	See the Bible, Genesis 2:9: 'the tree of life also in the midst of the garden, and the tree of knowledge of good and evil'
cormorant:	bird of prey. It is a bitter irony that Satan sits on the tree of life to plan mankind's death
lines 209–14:	See Genesis 2:8: 'And the Lord God planted a garden eastward in Eden'. Auran is about fifty miles south of Damascus and 'great Seleucia', so called to distinguish it from other cities of the same name built by Alexander's general, Seleucus, is south-east of Auran on the banks of the Tigris. Telassar, on the east bank of the Euphrates, is apparently an alternative site for Paradise; according to Isaiah 37:12, 'the children of Eden which were in Telassar' were destroyed utterly

lines 214–22:	A paraphrase of Genesis 2:9: 'And out of the ground made the Lord God to grow every tree that is pleasant to the sight, and good for food; the tree of life also in the midst of the garden, and the tree of knowledge of good and evil'
blooming:	causing to bloom (transitive). Ambrosia was the food of the gods
vegetable:	having the power of growth; 'animal', of growth and generation; 'rational', of growth, generation and reason
lines 223–46:	See Genesis 2:10: 'And a river went out of Eden to water the garden: and from thence it was parted, and became into four heads.' This river is identified by Milton in IX, 71–3 as the Tigris. It flowed through Eden and, when it reached the hill crowned by Paradise, part of it flowed straight through in an underground passage, while part was drawn up to form a fountain which irrigated the garden by means of channels. These then united to carry the water down the hillside to rejoin the river, which subsequently split up into four streams
shaggy:	covered with trees and bushes
kindly:	natural
diverse:	in all directions
sapphire:	light blue in colour
crisped:	ruffled by the breeze
orient:	lustrous
line 239:	'wandering courses beneath overhanging branches'
nectar:	the drink of the gods
nice:	over-precise
beds and curious knots:	flower-beds laid out in intricate designs
boon:	bounteous
Embrowned:	made shady (Italian *imbrunire*)
line 247:	'A spot of varied natural beauty'. A 'rural seat' would not mean a 'country house' to Milton
odorous gums:	aromatic resins
amicable:	delicious
Hesperian fables true:	if the classical stories about the Hesperides are to be believed. The Latin poet Ovid (43BC–AD17) tells, in *Metamorphoses*, IV, 637, of the gardens on an island in the western ocean, in which grew the golden apples which Hercules had to steal as one of his labours; they were guarded by the daughters of Hesperus, the Evening Star, and the dragon Ladon

irriguous: well-watered

line 256:   Since part of the curse pronounced on Adam (Genesis 3:18) was that the earth should bring forth thorns and thistles, the rose before the Fall was presumably without thorns. The thornless rose thus became a symbol of man's sinless state

umbrageous: shady

mantling: covering, as with a mantle

line 260:   Murmuring waters, soft breezes and harmonious birdsong are also features of Edmund Spenser's (1552?–99) Bower of Bliss in *The Faerie Queene*, II, 12, 171. For a discussion of Milton's description of Eden, see Commentary, pp. 61–3

apply: contribute, add

Pan: The name Pan means 'all' in Greek, and Pan here is the symbol of universal nature

Graces: three minor goddesses personifying the refining influences of life; the 'Hours' personified the seasons

lines 268–85:   This collection of comparisons underlines the superiority of Paradise by claiming that even the most celebrated gardens of ancient times could match it. The four unnamed rivers of Eden (line 233) are paralleled here by the rivers Orontes, Triton and Nile, and the Castalian spring

Proserpine: or Persephone (for Milton uses the Greek or Roman form of a proper name as best suits his need of the moment), daughter of Ceres, or Demeter, the goddess of agriculture and particularly corn, was picking flowers in a meadow at Enna, in central Sicily, when she was kidnapped by Dis, or Pluto, king of the underworld, and carried off underground. Ceres searched everywhere, neglecting the crops, and finally discovered where her daughter was. Pluto agreed to release Proserpine if no food had passed her lips; but, because she had eaten six pomegranate seeds, she must spend six winter months of every year with him and the joyful remainder of the year on earth

line 273:   The beautiful grove of Daphne beside the river Orontes near Antioch was watered by a stream named after the Castalian spring at Delphi; this was because there was an oracle sacred to Apollo in both places – hence 'inspired'

lines 275–9:	Milton here follows Diodorus Siculus, a Greek historian living in Sicily who wrote a history of the world in the first century BC. King Ammon of Libya (also known by classical writers – the Gentiles – as Libyan Jupiter, but here identified with Noah's son, Ham, Vulgate form Cham) fathered a child, Bacchus, on the maiden Amalthea. He hid them from his wife, Rhea, on Nysa, an island in the river Triton near Tunis; the ruddy-faced Bacchus, who became the god of wine, was also known as Dionysus from the name of the island
Abassin:	Abyssinian or Ethiopian. According to Milton's authority, the geographer and ecclesiastical historian Heylyn (1600–62), Mount Amara (which is actually a range rather than a single summit) was a smooth black rock a day's journey in height, on the top of which the sons of the emperors of Abyssinia were raised in careful seclusion. It was situated in the west of Ethiopia, not far from the source of the Nile, and Heylyn thought it to be very close to the Equator; for this reason it was believed to enjoy perpetual spring, and was claimed by many to be the true Paradise
head:	source

Book IV, lines 288–324

The human inhabitants of Paradise are now described: Adam and Eve, naked and without any sense of shame. Each surpasses all their descendants, but in different ways, and both recognise the innate superiority of Adam.

NOTES AND GLOSSARY:

erect:	repeated to stress their superiority over the beasts
native:	natural, not acquired
line 292:	See Genesis 1:27: 'So God created man in his own image'
whence:	from the godlike virtues listed in line 293
front:	forehead (Latin *frons*)
eye sublime:	confident gaze; not lowered in false humility
hyacinthine:	a Homeric epithet rather than an indication of the blue colour of the hyacinth; but in heraldry, hyacinth indicates tawny, a variety of brown very close to the colour of Milton's own hair. Milton may

well have created Adam in *his* own image. The length of Adam's close-curled hair is correct for a man of Milton's time – shoulder-length. Eve's more luxuriant tresses, like the tendrils of a vine, hang down to her waist. A marginal gloss to the Authorised Version of the Bible, I Corinthians 2:10, asserts that this covering of hair indicates that the wife is under the power of her husband

Dishevelled: hanging loose

Wanton: unrestrained

coy: shy. The word has come to imply an assumed modesty

honour dishonourable: an example of oxymoron, a figure of speech by which two words of opposite meaning are placed in juxtaposition (compare *precious bane* in I, 692). This code of false honour, created to cover a sense of shame man should never have felt, is contrasted with the native honour of his state of innocent nakedness in line 289 above

---

Book IV, lines 325–55

Having set Adam and Eve in their Paradise, Milton surrounds them with a kingdom of animals, all living in amity with one another and all content to acknowledge the supremacy of man.

NOTES AND GLOSSARY:

To recommend cool zephyr: to make the cool breeze acceptable

easy: luxurious

Nectarine: with juice tasting like nectar; but possibly the variety of peach called nectarine

compliant: need not mean 'pliant, easily bent' (Verity's note); Milton intends to imply that even the fruit-trees were eager to satisfy Adam's wishes

line 334: 'A grassy bank, soft as down, dotted with variegated flowers'

gentle purpose: innocent conversation

Wanted: were lacking

dalliance: caressing

lines 340–7: This lack of fear and enmity among the animals is in intentional contrast to the situation after the Fall, described in X, 710–14

ramped: sprang playfully

ounces: lynxes; used loosely of other felines also

pards:	leopards
lithe proboscis:	flexible trunk; poetic diction
Insinuating:	tying himself in folds, as complicated as the Gordian knot which Alexander the Great cut through with his sword
His braided train:	his patterned tail, or possibly the whole of his body behind the head
fatal guile:	even before he is possessed by Satan, the Serpent gives clear indications of his cunning nature; but they pass unnoticed
bedward ruminating:	chewing the cud on their way to rest
Ocean Isles:	to the West, in the Atlantic; probably the Azores, on the evidence of line 592 below
ascending scale:	The ascendant was the sign of the zodiac currently rising over the horizon. Since the sun was in Aries (III, 555–61), 'the stars that usher evening' would rise in Libra, the Scales, the sign opposite to Aries in the zodiac. Possibly a play upon the word 'scale'

Book IV, lines 356–408

Satan apostrophises Adam and Eve, not without some regret for the dire fate which he intends to bring upon them, but determined to use any means to wreak his vengeance upon God. Then, taking animal shape, he approaches them and lies in wait, seeking a suitable opportunity to do them harm.

NOTES AND GLOSSARY:

in gaze:	*At gaze* is a heraldic term, indicating the stillness and silence from which Satan now rouses himself
failed:	that had previously failed him
room:	place
other mould:	another substance. The fallen angels believed that man had been created to replace them; see II, 345–53
line 370:	'badly protected, considering how happy you are'
for heaven:	as a heaven
no purposed foe:	I have no intention of being your enemy
forlorn:	lost, defenceless
strait:	strict
all her kings:	See the Bible, Isaiah 14:9, 'Hell . . . hath raised up from their thrones all the kings of the nations'
lines 386–7:	'Blame him who forces me to take this revenge on you who do me no wrong instead of on him who has wronged me'
public reason:	reasons of state, which justify private injury. Here speaks Satan the politician

A lion:	See the Bible, I Peter 5:8: 'your adversary the devil, as a roaring lion, Walketh about, seeking whom he may devour'
purlieu:	land on the outskirts of a forest
straight:	straightaway
couches close:	hugs the ground, ready to spring

Book IV, lines 409–597

Adam and Eve discuss their relationship, and Eve relates how she first woke to life. Satan is so stung to envy of their happy state that his face betrays him to the watchful Uriel, who reports to Gabriel, captain of the guard on Eden, and then returns to his post on the sun.

NOTES AND GLOSSARY:

line 411:	'only partner and unique part'. Verbal repetition is a characteristic feature of Milton's style; see p. 67. Adam's speech is based on the first two chapters of the Bible, Genesis 1–2, whereas Eve's reply stressing Adam's superiority is taken from I Corinthians 11, in the New Testament of the Bible
possess:	inhabit
lines 432–3:	Milton has altered the word-order to emphasise 'one easy prohibition', 'let us not think one simple restriction difficult'
lines 440–3:	See I Corinthians 11:9: 'the woman' (was created) for the man'
flesh of my flesh:	See Genesis 2:23: 'This is ... flesh of my flesh'
head:	See I Corinthians 11:3: 'the head of the woman is the man'
Pre-eminent by so much odds:	superior to such an extent. Eve rejoices that she enjoys the love and protection of Adam, whereas he suffers the disadvantage of having no equal
liquid plain:	calm lake
lines 461–71:	Eve's admiration for her own reflection is reminiscent of Ovid's story of the youth Narcissus in *Metamorphoses* III, 417; he pined away for love of his own image. Eve, however, is led by God to the more substantial love of Adam, and this may well be an expression of Milton's view that a woman should direct her love towards her husband and not waste time on her own appearance
stays:	waits
platan:	plane-tree (Latin *platanus*)

line 483:   See Genesis 2:23: 'Adam said, "This is now bone of my bones, and flesh of my flesh"'

nearest my heart: from his left side, near his heart. Medieval commentators stressed that Eve could never have been Adam's equal, not having been taken from his head

line 486:   individual, undivided, inseparable

unreproved: innocent. Eve could look lovingly at Adam without ogling him

impregns: impregnates

line 503:   IX, 263–4 makes it clear that conjugal love excites Satan's envy more than anything else

plained: complained

Imparadised: placed in the paradise of each other's embrace, which is happier than Eden itself

pines: tortures

what I have gained: the secret of the tree of knowledge

lines 525–6:   See Genesis 3:5: 'in the day ye eat thereof . . . ye shall be as gods, knowing good and evil'

line 530:   'There is a chance that fortune may lead me'; a Miltonic quibbling repetition

roam: roaming

in utmost longitude: in the farthest west

Slowly: Because of the refractive index of the earth's atmosphere, the sun appears to descend more slowly as it approaches the earth's surface

right aspect: directly, at right angles; 'aspect' is a technical term describing the positional relationship of heavenly bodies. The setting sun shines horizontally from the west across the top of the plateau of Paradise and strikes the inside of the rocky wall at its eastern extremity

alablaster: the seventeenth-century spelling of 'alabaster', a white, veined marble

Gabriel: an angel of peace in the Bible. Milton would have had to go to earlier Jewish traditions to find him as a warrior

unarmed: in contrast to the fallen angels in II, 532–8

the even: the part already in darkness

thwarts: crosses; some editions 'thwart', across. Shooting stars were believed to be caused by the combustion of vapours exhaled from the earth and blown down again by the upper air, thus giving warning of strong winds to come

thy course by lot:	Offices in the Hebrew temple were apportioned by lot; but so, quite frequently, are such military offices as guard-duty
latest:	subsequent to the Son and the angels
described:	descried, perceived
his airy gait:	his course through the air
shade:	of trees
meridian hour:	noon
line 585:	Milton shared Gabriel's difficulty in knowing how to deal successfully with spiritual substance; battle-wounds (VI, 323-53) and how angels make love (VIII, 615-29) are two cases in point
slope downward:	The sun had dropped below the horizon during the preceding conversation, and Uriel could now return to his post *down* a beam stretching from Paradise
Azores:	in the far west
lines 592-5:	Milton shows his knowledge of both the Ptolemaic and Copernican systems of astronomy. If the sun goes round the earth, it has now sunk below the western horizon. If, on the other hand, it is the earth that moves, it will do so much more slowly, and will have turned in the opposite direction, lifting its Western horizon above the sun, whose light is still reflected on the clouds
Incredible how swift:	One of the arguments against Copernicanism was the incredible speeds it involved
Diurnal:	on its daily course
less voluble:	less swift to rotate on its axis

Book IV, lines 598-775

As night falls, Adam and Eve seek their rest. Having given thanks to God, they make love; and Milton writes a hymn of praise to their wedded love, the innocence of which is all too soon to be lost.

NOTES AND GLOSSARY:

livery:	'distinctive clothes' (definition given in the *Oxford English Dictionary*)
accompanied:	in the sense that a piano accompanies a solo instrument
descant:	variations on the melody
line 605:	living, uncut, in its natural state; as in II, 1049-50
Apparent:	made apparent, revealed
inclines:	weighs down

declares his dignity: Milton the Puritan believed firmly in the superiority of the active over the contemplative life (See his *Areopagitica*: 'I cannot praise a fugitive and cloistered virtue'), and he applies this to Adam

regard: watching over

scant manuring: ineffectual cultivation

Ask: require

author: she had sprung from his side

seasons: times of day: it was forever spring

Sweet is ... is sweet: The most striking example in *Paradise Lost* of epanalepsis, or repetition. See Commentary, p. 67

charm: probably a conscious play upon double derivation: Latin *carmen*, a song, and Old English *cyrm*, noise of birds. See also 'precious bane', I, 692

orient: eastern, as he is rising in the morning

solemn bird: the nightingale

general: of us all

darkness: the original darkness of Old Night, joint ruler with Chaos of the 'limitless profound' before hell or the universe were created. One of the functions of the stars is to keep this total darkness at bay

kindly: 'benign' rather than 'natural to them'

Divide the night: a translation of the Latin phrase *dividere noctem*, to divide the night into watches by blowing a trumpet to signal the changing of the guard

planter: See Genesis 2:8: 'God planted a garden'. The list of flowering things that follows is reminiscent of that other Miltonic flower passage, in *Lycidas* 139–51

jessamine: jasmine, as in *Lycidas*

flourished: crowned with flowers

Mosaic: a pattern of tiny coloured flowers

costliest emblem: richest inlaid work; but Milton must also have been aware of the currently popular emblem books, portraying such pictorial symbols as a pair of compasses – fidelity, in John Donne (1572–1631), – a mother pelican – self-sacrifice, in Richard Crashaw (c.1613–49), – and here such floral virtues as the humility of the violet

feigned: imagined by poets

lines 707–8: These three pastoral deities are very alike: they are all unsophisticated nature-gods, frequently represented as half man and half goat, and with a goat's lustfulness. Pan is the god of flocks and shepherds, Silvanus of woods, and Faunus of the fields

close:	secret
hymenean:	wedding-song, from the classical god of marriage, Hymen
genial:	nuptial (Latin *genialis*); Milton does not identify this angel. Adam in VIII, 484–7 tells Raphael that it was God who first brought Eve to him
lines 714–19:	The resemblance between Eve and Pandora (also beautiful but dangerous) had already been remarked by Milton in *The Doctrine and Discipline of Divorce* (Bohn III, 224). Prometheus (forethought) and Epimetheus (afterthought) were the sons of the Titan Iapetus. Prometheus stole fire from heaven to benefit mankind, and in revenge Zeus caused Hephaestus (Vulcan) to create a beautiful woman whom the gods endowed with gifts (hence her name, Pandora). Hermes led her to Epimetheus who, disregarding his brother's advice not to accept anything from Zeus, married her, and opened the casket she brought. All the gifts save one – hope – escaped and were lost to mankind for ever
event:	result
authentic:	original
starry pole:	the night sky. The words of the prayer echo the Bible, Psalm 74:16: 'The day is thine, the night also is thine: thou hast prepared the light and the sun'
fill the earth:	See Genesis 1:28: 'replenish the earth'. Generation was intended to take place in an unfallen Eden
lines 736–8:	Milton shows his dislike of religious ritual. In line 720 he had not made Adam and Eve *kneel* in prayer
Handed:	hand in hand
lines 741–7:	For a discussion of Milton's views on sexual relationships before the Fall, see Commentary, pp. 59–61
Mysterious:	symbolic (of the relationship between Christ and the Church?)
hypocrites:	those who insist on the necessity for celibacy in priests
commands to some:	1 Corinthians 7:1: 'It is good for a man not to touch a woman. Nevertheless, to avoid fornication, let every man have his own wife'
lines 750–65:	Milton's hymn in praise of wedded love is in keeping with Protestant tradition
sole propriety:	the only thing that Adam and Eve alone possess
charities:	natural affections

lines 763–5:	Cupid's golden shafts inspired love, his leaden ones repelled it. Lamps were usually symbols of inconstancy, extinguished by the slightest breeze, but Love's own lamp burns steadily, while his wings are both resplendent and regal
Mixed dances:	particularly obnoxious to the Puritans
mask:	masked ball, for one of which, *Comus*, the young Milton had himself written the libretto in 1634
starved:	unrequited
best quitted:	most suitably repaid
repaired:	made good the loss (with new roses)
know to know:	have the wisdom to seek to know

Book IV, lines 776–1015

Gabriel sends out his night-patrols through Paradise. One of these discovers Satan, in the form of a toad, seeking to bemuse the mind of the sleeping Eve. Satan is taken before Gabriel and, having considered resistance, decides against it, and leaves the garden in defeat – for the time being.

NOTES AND GLOSSARY:

lines 776–7:	The earth casts a cone of shadow on the side opposite to the sun. When the axis of this cone reaches the meridian, it is midnight, but it does not do this until the last line of Book IV. It is now 'halfway up', that is, it is nine o'clock, the beginning of the second of the four equal watches of the night (line 688); the first began at sunset (lines 539–43)
full west:	in the extreme west, since they were starting from the eastern end of Paradise
shield and spear:	old military terms for 'left' and 'right'
these:	the troop under his own command
secure:	without fear
Who:	someone who (Uriel)
these:	Ithuriel and Zephon
Squat:	squatting
line 805:	Before the system of circulation of the blood in the human body was discovered by William Harvey (1578–1657), the heart was regarded not as a pump but as an oven, warming and vitalising the cold air provided by the lungs and sending it outward along the arteries to nourish the extremities of the body. This blood spreading from the heart was called 'spiritual blood', and the heart itself was the centre

of *virtus spiritualis* or *vitalis* ('pure blood'); *virtus naturalis* was situated in the liver, and *virtus animalis* ('animal spirits') in the brain. Pure blood gave strength to the animal spirits which fed the controlling brain; and it was through these animal spirits that the human mind could, it was believed, be influenced by external forces

distempered: disordered
temper: a weapon that has been tempered
nitrous: containing saltpetre, an ingredient of gunpowder
Fit for the tun: ready to be packed in barrels
Against: in preparation for
obscure: dark and unknown
shape: visible form
pined: mourned
half-rounding guards: each of the two squadrons had completed its semicircular patrol, and they had met at the western extremity of Paradise
shade: trees
of regal port: of royal bearing. Unlike the lower-ranking Zephon, Gabriel recognises Satan, despite his changed appearance
charge: task, commission
line 880: 'who were not in favour of following your example by sinning'
Dole: grief
object: raise as an objection (to our leaving hell without permission)
durance: imprisonment
thus much what was asked: so much in answer to your question
lines 904–5: 'What a great judge of what is and is not wise we have lost since Satan fell from Heaven'
Gravely in doubt: Gabriel is heavily sarcastic
However: in whatever way he can
line 925: 'I have not sought to escape because my powers of endurance are less than those of the others'
stood thy fiercest: either (1) withstood thy fiercest assaults; or (2) was always thy fiercest opponent in the battle
vollied thunder: volleys of thunder unleashed by Messiah during the war in heaven, VI, 836
at random: unconsidered. Satan claims that Gabriel does not appreciate, as he does, what the leader of a beaten army must *not* do: risk everything on a course of action he has not himself tried out

Fame:	rumour (Latin *fama*)
afflicted powers:	beaten armies
in mid air:	The devils supposedly controlled the middle region of the air, where storms were generated
put to:	forced to; Satan's new plan of settlement will inevitably encounter resistance
gay:	fine (ironical)
line 945:	To bow at fixed intervals before God's throne is an easier alternative than maintaining intervals in battle-formation
traced:	discovered
engaged:	promised
aread:	counsel
avaunt:	get thee gone!
facile:	easily passed
limitary:	guarding the boundary
thy wings:	in VI, 771, Messiah rides on the wings of the cherubim
road of heaven:	the Milky Way, according to VII, 579
phalanx:	military formation, of a crescent moon whose horns close in round Satan
ported:	slanted across the left breast, ready to be brought down to the charging position
lines 980–5:	Epic simile. 'Ceres', the goddess of agriculture (see line 271), here stands for corn, probably barley since it is 'bearded'
careful:	anxious, in case the sheaves from which he hopes so much yield chaff, not corn
dilated:	The devils have the power to expand or contract at will
Teneriff:	a mountain on the Canary Island of the same name, wrongly believed to be fabulously high
Atlas:	perhaps the Libyan range which supposedly supports the sky, or the cloud-capped mountain in Mauretania believed in classical times to be one of the pillars of the sky
unremoved:	immovable
cope:	canopy, firmament
all the elements:	the whole universe
wrack:	wreck, destruction
golden scales:	God weighed many things: the elements used in the Creation; rulers, such as Belshazzar, who in Daniel 5:27 is weighed and found wanting; and here the consequences to Satan of retreating or fighting.

God decides that Satan shall retreat, so that he may be free to tempt Adam and Eve again, uninfluenced by irresistible force. Only thus will man's obedience have real meaning. The scales are remembered in the seventh zodiacal sign of Libra, between Virgo ('Astrea') and 'Scorpio', which reaches its zenith at midnight

pendulous: hanging from heaven on a golden chain

ponders: weighs

sequel: consequence – to Satan

kicked the beam: a phrase describing the violent action whereby one arm of the balance, on the lighter side, flies up and strikes the crossbeam sharply

look up: they look up to Libra in its zenith; the time is therefore midnight, when the shades of night begin to flee (see note to lines 776–7), not dawn. It expressly states in IX, 58 that Satan fled 'by night'

His mounted scale aloft: that he was destined to lose

nor more: he said no more

Book IX, lines 1–47

This is the key book of the poem, the book of man's fall. Milton begins it by claiming that such a theme is suitable for a heroic poem, and is in fact more fitting than the subject of any previous epic poem. He expresses the hope that he will prove equal to the task.

NOTES AND GLOSSARY:

lines 1–5:   The four preceding books have been concerned with friendly talk between Adam and the archangel Raphael, covering the Creation, the War in heaven, and various cosmic questions posed by Adam. Now this social intercourse is ended for ever, forfeited by sinful man

Venial: harmless, innocent

breach: break-up of the hitherto friendly relationship

distance and distaste: cooling-off and aversion

a world of: a vast amount of. A quibble on two meanings of 'world'; compare line 648

argument: subject, theme

lines 14–19:   Milton selects significant incidents from the great classical epics. From *Iliad* 22, Achilles' vindictive pursuit of Hector round the walls of Troy. From the *Aeneid*, the wrath of Turnus, for two reasons: he loses Lavinia unjustly, and this again shows the hero of the epic in a suitably unfavourable light; and human anger is once more the theme. But not merely human anger is surpassed in Milton's own epic, but the wrath of the pagan gods: despite the opposition of Neptune (Poseidon), Odysseus returns home after ten years of wandering in the *Odyssey*, and Aeneas, son of Cytherea (Venus), survives the anger of Juno to found Rome. God's anger is more terrible – and more epic – than any of these

answerable: suitably elevated. The grandeur of Milton's style is one of his most remarkable epic characteristics

celestial patroness: Milton's Christian equivalent of the epic poet's pagan muse has been directly invoked in the opening of each of three preceding sections of *Paradise Lost*: I, 1–26; III, 1–55; and VII, 1–7

nightly: Milton composed his poetry in bed and had it written down for later revision. The adjectives 'unimplored' and 'unpremeditated' underline the inspirational nature of his creative process

first: the first lines of *Paradise Lost* were written down about 1642; see note to IV, 32

long choosing: Milton spent years considering the genre, hero, and even the language for his proposed great work; see his *Reason of Church Government* (Bohn II, 478–9)

beginning late: a natural consequence of this long choosing, superimposed upon the late maturing of his genius which Milton himself remarks in his twenty-third birthday sonnet, 'my late spring no bud or blossom sheweth'

sedulous: diligent, assiduous

indite: write formally of

mastery: art, skill

to dissect: writers of both Classical and Italian Romantic epics went into great detail in describing wounds inflicted in battle

races and games: a feature of Classical epic, tournaments were a feature of Romantic epic

tilting furniture: paraphernalia of jousting

emblazoned: with a heraldic device on it

Impresses: heraldic devices on shields, sometimes with mottoes

caparisons: decorative trappings (of a horse)

Bases: short protective metal skirts worn by mounted knights

feast:	The duties of the various officials at a mediaeval banquet were as follows: the marshal seated the guests according to their rank; the sewer marched in before the meats and supervised their serving; while the seneschal acted as the household steward. Milton calls all this highly organised system of tournament, heraldry and feasting 'artifice', and dismisses it as beneath the dignity of true epic.
Me ... Remains:	an imitation of the Latin *me manet*
That name:	Milton's subject matter is not merely worthy of epic; it will enhance the reputation of epic poetry itself, unless one or all of three dangers materialise: it is too late in the world's history for epic to flourish; England is too far north for the climate to favour its creation; Milton himself at over fifty may be too old. But Milton hopes that the inspiration of his Heavenly Muse will compensate for these disadvantages
line 45:	In three of his four invocations in *Paradise Lost*, Milton speaks of his inspiration as 'winged'; see also III, 13 and VII, 4

Book IX, lines 48–191

The story of Satan, broken off at the end of Book IV, is now resumed. Having circled the Earth in continuous darkness for seven nights to observation, he returns to Eden. He selects the guileful serpent as the most fitting instrument for his purpose, and, after a soliloquy in which he seeks to justify the evil he intends to perpetrate, he enters the body of the serpent and waits for morning.

NOTES AND GLOSSARY:

short arbiter:	the brief period of twilight holds the balance between day and night
Night's hemisphere:	Before the Fall, the poles of the earth's sphere were perpendicular, so that one half of the globe was in sunlight and half in darkness. Satan contrives to fly in continuous darkness for seven nights by two methods: for three nights he flies due west, keeping ahead of the rising sun; on two of the other nights he flies from north to south along a meridian that is in darkness, crossing the pole at dawn and flying north again along the reverse meridian, which is just beginning its twelve-hour period of night. The great

circles he flies along are the 'colures', the meridians which pass through the equinoctial and the solstitial points of the ecliptic and intersect one another at right angles at the poles, dividing the earth's globe into four equal segments

improved: Satan has perfected his plan during his long flight

maugre: in spite of

heavier: heavier punishment

By night he fled: this confirms the time-sequence suggested in the note to IV, 1010

averse from: opposite to

line 71: Milton here identifies one of the four rivers of Paradise (IV, 223) as the Tigris

rising mist: the spray caused by the underground river shooting up in a fountain into the garden. Satan, following the course of the underground river, enters the garden hidden in the spray

lines 76–83: Milton supplements his astronomical account of Satan's journey with a geographical account of his nocturnal wanderings. He had flown from Eden over 'Pontus', the Black Sea, and 'the pool Maeotis', the Sea of Azov. On across Russia to 'the river Ob', which flows into the Arctic Ocean; so across the north pole and down as far on the other side to the Antarctic and the south pole. From east to west Satan flew from the Syrian river Orontes to Darien, the Isthmus of Panama, which puts a bar across the ocean; on across the Pacific into Asia and so back over India, crossing first the Ganges and then the more westerly Indus

pool: inland sea

deep: very careful

sentence: decision

suggestions: temptations

Doubt: suspicion

officious: fulfilling their office (Latin *officiosus*)

gradual: in ascending steps. The vegetable soul has the power of growth: the sensitive soul of growth and sensation: and the rational soul of growth, sensation, and reason

hateful siege of contraries: the opposition between the pleasures outside Satan and the pain within. If he were to return to Heaven, where the joys are greater still, his pain would be the greater

lines 126–9:	Satan's pain is not lessened by making others unhappy, but he does find some relief in destroying
Follow:	fall after him
almighty styled:	Although God is called 'Almighty', it took Him six days to create the new world; it will take Satan only one to destroy it
in one night:	the night of Satan's rebellion in Heaven. Satan claims that he attracted almost half the angelic host to his banner, whereas the more usual estimate is one-tenth (leaving nine orders of angels). Satan also maintains that God's plan to create man and his universe to fill the gap made by the devils' defection was born that night
name:	race (Latin *nomen*)
lines 145–51:	Satan cannot decide whether God determined to make good his angelic losses with replacements created from Earth to increase the devils' humiliation or because He had used up all the spiritual essence when He first created the angels
indignity:	To add insult to injury, God has detailed bands of angels to guard and care for this earthborn creation
flaming ministers:	the cherubim
constrained:	forced to enter into the confines of a beast
line 166:	'To change this spiritual essence into flesh and become a brute'
obnoxious:	exposed to (Latin *obnoxius*)
reck:	care
light:	land, find its mark
higher I fall short:	I cannot harm the higher target, God. Satan repeats his claim that God made man out of dust to spite the fallen angels
labyrinth:	maze of intricate folds
horrid shade:	dreadful dark corner
nocent:	harmful
grassy herb:	poetic diction
in at his mouth:	because the soul was supposed to enter and leave the body through the mouth
act intelligential:	power of intelligent action
close:	concealed

Book IX, lines 192–411

Adam and Eve waken in Paradise to a new day. Eve suggests that they divide their labours to increase productivity. Adam is unwilling to leave her unprotected, but grudgingly yields when Eve complains that he finds her unworthy of trust. They separate, and Eve is left, all unwitting, open to Satan's attack

NOTES AND GLOSSARY:

sacred light: Milton calls light 'holy' in III, 1. 1 John 1:51, 'God is light'. This whole passage is intended to imply a contrast between natural worship and the Church ritual which Milton and the Puritans abhorred

partake the season prime: enjoy the early morning hour. Prime was the period between 6 and 9 in the morning, and there is a play upon words here between 'prime', the hour, and 'prime', the very best

commune: discuss

dispatch: output

derides: makes mockery of

spring: grove

redress: tie so that they grow up straight

intermits: interrupts

motioned: proposed ('to make a motion' in a meeting)

not the lowest end: the highest aim. Smiles spring from love and love from reason, the great divider between man and the beasts

from wilderness: from becoming a wilderness

Or this or worse: whether this, or something worse, be his first design

seemliest: most fittingly

virgin: chaste

the parting angel: Raphael, who delivered his warning as he was leaving

firmness: steadfastness

lines 288–9: These thoughts which Adam has entertained are unworthy thoughts

entire: free from

diffident: untrusting

asperses: charges, though falsely. It is unpleasant even for the innocent to be spattered with filth

Access: increase

unite: join strength to virtue

Less: too little

straitened: restricted

line 328: 'By tempting us our enemy insults us with his low opinion of our virtue'

front: brow (Latin *frons*); also a quibble on *affronts* in line 328

event:	result, which has been witnessed by an approving Heaven
line 335:	This line expresses a sentiment dear to Milton – that virtue must be tested to be truly worth while; see *Aereopagitica* (Bohn II, 68)
Alone:	this increases the merit of virtue purified by trial
line 339:	'Just as safe whether we are alone or together'
no Eden:	no place of happiness
still erect:	always alert
mind:	a play upon words: 'remind' and 'take notice of'
suborned:	perverted to evil purposes
approve:	give proof of
attest:	bear witness to. If Eve resists temptation by herself, who will there be to substantiate her claim?
securer:	over confident, less well prepared. Adam tells Eve that if, after his warning, she feels better prepared to overcome temptation by going out to look for it, perhaps she had better do it rather than wait for temptation to come upon her unawares. Nor does he wish to force her to stay against her will
submiss though last:	submission in bearing, but having the last word
So bent:	having failed to overcome the weaker opponent
dryads:	wood-nymphs
oreads:	mountain-nymphs. The nymphs attended on Diana, here called Delia because of her birthplace on the island of Delos, who was the goddess of the hunt. Eve, who surpasses Diana in bearing and deportment, carries primitive gardening tools in place of a bow and quiver of arrows
Guiltless of fire:	fire had not been used in fashioning them. There is some suggestion here of Prometheus' 'guilt' in stealing fire from heaven to benefit mankind
lines 393–6:	Eve most closely resembled Pales, the Roman goddess of pastures; or Pomona, goddess of fruit-trees, whose seduction by Vertumnus is described in Ovid's *Metamorphoses* XIV, 771; or Ceres the goddess of agriculture, in the days before Jove fathered Proserpina upon her (see IV, 269–72). All were deities of cultivation
line 402:	'She promised to have everything ready'. The verb 'engaged' governs each of the succeeding lines as separate direct objects – an example of zeugma
hapless:	unfortunate
Event perverse:	the outcome was the opposite of what was expected

Book IX, lines 412–833

Satan, in serpent form, has been seeking Adam and Eve since dawn, hoping to find Eve alone. Against all expectation, he does indeed spy her alone, and approaches her, seeking to attract her attention by his movements and addressing her with fawning words. Amazed by his power of speech, Eve asks him how this has come about, and the serpent shows her the tree of knowledge as his source of speech. After an initial refusal to eat of the fruit, Eve succumbs to the temptation of becoming the equal, not merely of Adam but of a god; she eats, and the whole earth groans in agony. Out of fear of being destroyed and leaving Adam to some other woman, Eve decides to share the fruit with him, and goes to seek him.

NOTES AND GLOSSARY:

Mere serpent: just a serpent. Milton does not agree with those who would give Satan a cherub's face on a snake's body, or maintain that the temptation was all in Eve's mind

whole included race: all humanity was at that time included in Adam and Eve

tendance: tending. They tended the garden-plots, and planted the groves

his hap: his good fortune

voluble and bold: progressing openly with an undulating movement

Embordered: planted out as a border

hand: handiwork

feigned: told in story

Or of revived Adonis: either of Adonis, who, after being slain by a boar, supposedly returned each spring in a growth-ritual; referred to by Milton under his name of Thammuz in I, 446–52

renowned Alcinous: the gardens of Alcinous, king of the Phaeacians and host of Odysseus ('old Laertes' son') made famous by Homer in *Odyssey* VIII, 112–35

not mystic: not mythical, but biblical

sapient king: Solomon, the wise king, who 'took Pharaoh's daughter and brought her into the city of David' (See the Bible, 1 Kings 3:1), and who, according to the Bible, Song of Solomon 6:2, was a garden-lover

he: Satan

annoy: make noisome. Milton was very aware of the pollution in London that led to the Great Plague of 1665

tedded grass:	cut grass spread out to dry into hay
for her:	because of her
plat:	flat patch of ground
air:	mannerism
with rapine sweet bereaved:	robbed with gentle rape
gratulating:	congratulating himself on finding Eve alone
opportune:	open, exposed
of terrestrial mould:	formed from Earth
The way:	the method Satan intends to adopt is to disguise his hatred under an appearance of adoration
tend:	turn my attention
indented wave:	Creatures that hug the ground push themselves forward, drawing in their rear ends in folds, and then pushing forward once more. The serpent has only progressed in this manner since the Fall (Genesis 3:14); before that time, he held himself upright, resting his body on his curled round tail, as Milton here clearly describes
surging maze:	undulating labyrinth of coils
Crested aloft:	surmounted by his head, like a crest
carbuncle:	a precious stone, appropriately red in colour
verdant:	shining; usually applied to the fresh greenness of grass, as in 'verdant pastures'
spires:	coils
redundant:	flowing over one another
lines 504–10:	Milton stresses the serpent's beauty by his customary method of drawing on his vast classical learning to provide a list of celebrated serpents, none of whom, he says, could compare with the serpent in Paradise. See also IV, 268–75; IX 439–42. The serpents here intended are: those into which Cadmus, king of Thebes and reputed inventor of the alphabet, and his wife Harmonia (Hermione) were changed (Ovid's *Metamorphoses*, IV, 562–602); Aesculapius, god of medicine, worshipped in Epidaurus in the form of a serpent and who saved Rome in time of pestilence according to *Metamorphoses*, XV, 622–744. Jupiter Ammon or Libyan Jove was reputedly the father of Alexander the Great by Olympias, and as Jupiter Capitolinus of Scipio Africanus – in serpent form
to which:	those into which
tract:	course
wanton:	playful, intended to attract

line 522:	Homer in *Odyssey* X tells how the enchantress Circe bewitched the followers of Odysseus and changed them into swine, obedient to her call
turret:	towering
enamelled:	smooth and of varied colours
lines 529–30:	Satan, lacking the organs of speech, either used his tongue for the purpose, or projected impulses through the air, which then made noises like a human voice
single:	I alone among the creatures
shallow:	lacking profound intelligence. Satan flatters Eve by claiming that her rural setting is unworthy of her, and that she merits the adoration of multitudes and not merely the love of Adam alone: above all, she should be a goddess, not a human being
glozed:	flattered
proem:	prelude, introduction (to his temptation)
speakable of mute:	capable of speech from being dumb. Seventeenth-century commentators were exceedingly sceptical of Eve's simplicity in allowing her superior reason to be overcome by the serpent's flattery. Milton at least makes her ask the serpent how he came by this amazing power of speech – though intelligence in animals she had never doubted
abject thoughts:	unelevated, limited; as opposed to the 'speculations high or deep' of line 602
fennel:	a favourite food of snakes, this plant is supposed to encourage the annual casting of their skins. Snakes are also fond of sucking the teats of ewes and goats
tend their play:	the young animals continue to play instead of coming to their mothers to feed
utmost reach:	Milton's God had made sure that it would require a conscious decision by Adam or Eve to pluck the forbidden fruit
to degree:	to the extent of giving me the power of reason and the power of speech; the changes were 'inward', for to outward appearance he is still a serpent
Wanted not long:	was not lacking for long
middle:	the middle air, between Earth and Heaven
importune:	importunate, presumptuous
spirited:	possessed by a spirit; but there may be a quibble on the secondary meaning of 'bold'
proved:	put to the test. Eve doubts the virtue of a fruit which can inspire such unreasonable over-praise

lines 622–4:	A great deal of fruit will remain unpicked until men increase in number to match what has been provided for them, and there are more hands to take from nature what she has borne ('her birth')
blowing:	blossoming
balm:	the balsam tree
lines 634–42:	Satan as guide is compared in this epic simile to the *ignis fatuus* (Latin) or will-o'-the-wisp ('wandering fire') which was supposed to be an evil spirit that lighted unwary travellers to their death in swamps. It is, more prosaically, caused by the spontaneous combustion of methane, or marsh-gas
Compact of:	composed of
unctuous:	heavy and greasy
environs round:	encases

Kindled through agitation: set alight by constant movement

Fruitless:	useless; a quibble on *fruit* and *fruitless*; compare line 11

daughter of his voice: a voice from Heaven; a Hebraism

the rest:	for the rest
guilefully:	because he already knew of God's command. The ensuing dialogue is a paraphrase of Genesis 3:1–3
New part puts on:	assumes a new character – one of indignant defence of mankind. Milton imagines Satan as acting a part, reinforcing his words with movements ('Fluctuates disturbed') like an actor ('in act raised')
lines 670–6:	Epic simile
since mute:	oratory flourished in the ancient democracies with men such as Demosthenes, but has since been silenced

in himself collected: completely master of himself; Italian *in se raccolto*

audience:	attention
in highth:	plunging headlong into his subject, using every device of the actor's art to reinforce his oratory. Milton's customary spelling
zeal of right:	enthusiasm for a just cause
Mother of science:	fount of knowledge
To:	in addition to
not feared then:	therefore not to be feared
line 702:	Eve's fear of being struck dead has started a train of thought that must end with the removal of that same fear: if eating the fruit increases her knowledge of good, she will be a better and happier woman; if it increases her knowledge of evil, she will be

forewarned what to avoid, and will thereby also be better. God cannot in justice slay her for improving herself; and if He is God, He must be just; if not just, He cannot be God, and is therefore to be neither feared nor obeyed

proportion meet: just as I have risen a grade, from brute to human (for I am a man inside – 'internal man' – though still a serpent to outward appearance), so you will rise from human to divine. Perhaps a sort of death will indeed take place: a woman must die, that a goddess may be born

participating: sharing

if they: 'produce' understood

Impart: provide

lines 730–1: 'These and many other arguments indicate your mood'

Goddess humane: 'human goddess' is tempting; but 'benevolent, gracious' is the meaning in both II, 109 and *Paradise Regained*, I, 221

impregned: impregnated, filled with

to her seeming: as it seemed to her

Inclinable: inviting

elocution: the power of speech

after-bands: subsequent bonds

author unsuspect: informer above suspicion

lines 773–4: 'If I am being kept in ignorance of good and evil, how can I know *what* is to be feared?'

all: all ignorance

virtue: power

eating: that she was eating

boon: gay

precious: most prized. Eve uses positives for superlatives here

lines 796–7: 'Blessed in your operation to the extent of conferring wisdom'

infamed: uncelebrated

early care: first concern

others: God

Experience: willingness to put to the test

secret . . . secret: secluded . . . hidden from view

safe: not dangerous; like the safety-catch on a shotgun

odds of knowledge: the advantage that my new knowledge gives me

Confirmed: confirmed in my decision to include Adam – in case she is destroyed and he given another woman

Book IX, lines 834–1045

Eve seeks out Adam, and tells him what she has done. Horrified at first, eventually Adam decides to share her fate, whatever it may be. They eat the fruit and become inflamed with carnal lust, which they proceed to satisfy, finally falling asleep exhausted.

NOTES AND GLOSSARY:

sciential:	with the power of conferring knowledge
divine of:	with a premonition of
faltering measure:	the uneven beating of his apprehensive heart
downy smiled:	looked pleasantly covered with blossom. To Adam, it is still just another branch
ambrosial:	as of divine food; a bitter irony
apology to prompt:	Eve's expression was visible before she spoke, but it remained on her face in support of her speech of self-justification ('apologia'), like a prompter in a play. Milton had used theatrical imagery in lines 670–6
danger tasted:	danger if tasted
to admiration:	to an admirable extent
equal lot:	the same fate
line 887:	Eve's flushed cheeks reflect her inner disturbance
amiable:	delicious, as in IV, 250
line 901:	This alliterative line sums up Eve's degradation: her physical beauty has been ravaged; she has lost her air of innocence; and she is doomed to destruction
line 907:	Adam's motive in sinning is much nobler than Eve's (as might be expected from Milton); he would rather die with her than live without her
sweet converse:	soon to give way to bitter recrimination as the soul irrational through anger takes over from the soul irrational through lust. See p. 52
yet so:	even so
fact:	deed (Latin *factum*, 'that which has been done')
foretasted:	previously tasted by the serpent
Proportional ascent:	The argument advanced by the serpent in lines 710–12
prime creatures:	foremost creations
line 945:	'It is not to be thought of that God...'
Certain to:	resolved to, as in line 907
Direct or by occasion:	directly or indirectly
oblige:	render liable to punishment (Latin *obligare*)
event:	result

fondly:	foolishly
second groan:	the first had been when Eve tasted the fruit, lines 882–4
iterate:	repeat
swim and mirth:	Adam and Eve behave as though they are on drugs. The illusion that one can fly is a feature of hallucinogenic drug LSD
elegant:	refined
line 1019:	Milton here calls attention to his verbal quibble: both 'sapience', discernment, and 'savour', tastiness, derive ultimately from the same Latin verb, *sapere*
purveyed:	provided
For:	instead of
meet:	fitting
to:	caress
asphodel:	the lily of the Elysian fields; the name is preserved in its descendant, 'daffodil'
solace of their sin:	temporary sexual satisfaction is the only compensation for their crime

---

Book IX, lines 1046–189

Adam and Eve wake to a new sense of shame, and speedily cover their nakedness with figleaves. They quarrel bitterly, each blaming the other for the unhappy state in which they now find themselves.

NOTES AND GLOSSARY:

fallacious:	deceiving
bland:	pleasing the senses
unkindly fumes:	unnatural vapours
conscious:	guilty
lines 1057–9:	Shame covered them as with a robe, but uncovered them even more because it made them curious of their nakedness
lines 1059–62:	Epic simile. Samson, son of Manoah of the tribe of Dan ('the Danite'), was the strong man of the Hebrews, as Hercules was of the Greeks, and harassed the Philistines sorely. The Philistines bribed Delilah to persuade Samson to reveal the secret of his strength, which lay in his unshorn hair; this he eventually did, and was captured and blinded. Milton tells the story of Samson's last days in *Samson Agonistes*
constrained:	forced, unnatural

line 1067:	There is a verbal quibble here on 'evil' and 'Eve', who is not named in Genesis until after the Fall and from whose name some commentators think the word 'evil' is derived
worm:	serpent
lines 1078–80:	From their lust, a whole set of evils would follow; shame they are currently experiencing, and may be sure of suffering others: 'last' in line 1079 is rendered 'least' by Fowler but 'greatest' by Verity, but the sense is possibly of time ('most recent'), not size
umbrage:	shade
brown:	dark
obnoxious:	used by Milton in its Latin sense of 'being liable to' (*obnoxius*)
line 1101:	The 'fig-tree' is not, as Milton points out, the European fruit-bearing variety, but that which flourishes in India, the banyan; Milton makes the 'Decan' (the Deccan, the southern peninsula) stand for the whole of India, including Malabar, the south-western coast. His source was most probably Gerard's *Herball* (1597), itself based on Pliny's *Natural History (Historia Naturalis,* AD77), where the banyan, which does indeed propagate itself in the manner here described but has small leaves, is confused with the banana or plantain tree
Amazonian targe:	shield of Amazons, the women warriors of the Classics
of late:	over a century and a half earlier, in 1492, but recently in comparison to the date of the Fall
feathered cincture:	girdled by a feathered skirt
line 1132:	Adam here is sadly changed from the prelapsarian Adam in both appearance ('estranged in look') and in tone of speech ('altered style')
approve:	give proof of
conclude:	draw the conclusion, be sure
the head:	see note to IV, 443
facile:	easily persuaded
fair:	approvingly
expressed immutable:	shown to be unchangeable (by choosing death with you rather than life alone)
secure:	over-confident
brook:	endure

Part 3

Commentary

Miltonic epic

The evolution of epic poetry has already been sketched in Part I
(pp. 11–13); but Milton's own concept of the nature of epic and the
character of the epic hero must now be examined in greater detail with
reference to Books IV and IX, for these two books – Book IX
particularly – are primarily concerned with these topics.

In a famous passage at the beginning of Book IX (analysed in detail in
these notes, pp. 35–7), Milton rejects as inferior the themes of earlier
epics:

> I now must change
> Those notes to tragic; foul distrust, and breach
> Disloyal on the part of man, revolt,
> And disobedience: on the part of heaven
> Now alienated, distance and distaste,
> Anger and just rebuke, and judgment given,
> That brought into this world a world of woe,
> Sin and her shadow Death, and Misery
> Death's harbinger: sad task, yet argument
> Not less but more heroic than the wrath
> Of stern Achilles on his foe pursued
> Thrice fugitive about Troy wall; or rage
> Of Turnus for Lavinia disespoused,
> Or Neptun's ire or Juno's, that so long
> Perplexed the Greek and Cytherea's son;
> If answerable style I can obtain
> Of my celestial patroness, who deigns
> Her nightly visitation unimplored,
> And dictates to me slumbering, or inspires
> Easy my unpremeditated verse:
> Since first this subject for heroic song
> Pleased me long choosing, and beginning late;
> Not sedulous by nature to indite
> Wars, hitherto the only argument
> Heroic deemed, chief mastery to dissect
> With long and tedious havoc fabled knights

In battles feigned; the better fortitude
Of patience and heroic martyrdom
Unsung; or to describe races and games,
Or tilting furniture, emblazoned shields,
Impresses quaint, caparisons and steeds;
Bases and tinsel trappings, gorgeous knights
At joust and tournament; then marshalled feast
Served up in hall with sewers, and seneschals;
The skill of artifice or office mean,
Not that which justly gives heroic name
To person or to poem. Me of these
Nor skilled nor studious, higher argument
Remains, sufficient of itself to raise
That name, unless an age too late, or cold
Climate, or years damp my intended wing
Depressed, and much they may, if all be mine,
Not hers who brings it nightly to my ear.

(IX, 5–47)

Milton's approach to epic is not, however, a negative one. He does not merely reject earlier epic patterns – and, indeed, retains much of the machinery of Classical epic, like Homeric similes and invocations to his Muse; he has a positive doctrine to put in its place. And this doctrine must be presented in a suitably elevated style to match the grandeur of its subject.

Milton's epic doctrine is one of Temperance, or self-control. He arrived at it by synthesising a number of influences: the Classical philosophies he had so thoroughly studied during his years of reading at Horton – Stoicism, Aristotelianism, and especially, Platonism; the example of his one acknowledged poetic master, Edmund Spenser (1552?–99), particularly in Book II of *The Faerie Queene*, the book of Sir Guyon, personification of temperance; and his own Puritan temperament, which caused him to reject the contemplative life in favour of the active life of the true warfaring Christian, active on the field of battle, but the battlefield of the spirit:

I cannot praise a fugitive and cloistered virtue unexercised and unbreathed, that never sallies out and seeks her adversary, but slinks out of the race, where that immortal garland is to be run for, not without dust and heat. Assuredly we bring not innocence into the world, we bring impurity much rather; that which purifies us is trial, and trial is by what is contrary. That virtue therefore which is but a youngling in the contemplation of evil, and knows not the utmost that vice promises to her followers, and rejects it, is but a blank virtue, not a pure; her whiteness is but an excremental whiteness; which was the reason why our sage and serious poet Spenser, (whom I dare be known to think a better teacher than Scotus or Aquinas*) describing true temperance under the person of Guion, brings him in with his palmer through the cave of Mammon, and the bower of earthly bliss, that he might see and know, and yet abstain.

(*Areopagitica*, Bohn II, 68)

The warfaring Puritan here described is very like the Platonic rational soul. When this soul beholds beauty, it generalises it and loves it without reference to and in preference to its origin in human flesh; this abstract Beauty is an aspect of divinity and so, through its contemplation, the rational soul achieves union with the divine One, whom the Christian neo-Platonists of the Renaissance identified with God. But there is not only the rational soul, but two irrational souls also: the soul irrational through lust, which seeks to possess human beauty carnally; and the soul irrational through anger, which seeks to destroy it. In Book II of *The Faerie Queene*, Guyon is attacked for the first six cantos by angry knights; but he is in much greater danger from the attempted seductions of the lustful Acrasia and the charms of the beauties in the Bower of Bliss, for, as Spenser observes, 'The strong through pleasure soonest falls, the weak through smart' (II, 1, 57). Milton was to develop this theme in *Samson Agonistes*, but Adam too is 'fondly overcome with female charm' (IX, 999). Eve herself realises that a direct attack by their unknown enemy does not constitute the greater danger:

His violence though fear'st not, being such,
As we, not capable of death or pain,
Can either not receive, or can repel.
His fraud is then thy fear.

(IX, 282–5)

To Milton, Adam's original sin is not so much disobedience as intemperance – as it had been Satan's and was to be Samson's; the effect of eating the fatal fruit is the onset of sensuality:

So said he, and forbore not glance or toy
Of amorous intent, well understood
Of Eve, whose eye darted contagious fire.
Her hand he seized, and to a shady bank,
Thick overhead with verdant roof embowered
He led her nothing loth; flowers were the couch,
Pansies, and violets, and asphodel,
And hyacinth, earth's freshest softest lap.
There they their fill of love and love's disport
Took largely, of their mutual guilt the seal,

*Thomas Aquinas and Duns Scotus were thirteenth-century scholastic philosophers.

The solace of their sin, till dewy sleep
Oppressed them, wearied with their amorous play.

(IX, 1034–45)

When they awake, the soul irrational through anger takes over from the soul irrational through lust:

They sat them down to weep, nor only tears
Rained at their eyes, but high winds worse within
Began to rise, high passions, anger, hate,
Mistrust, suspicion, discord, and shook sore
Their inward state of mind, calm region once
And full of peace, now tossed and turbulent:
For understanding ruled not, and the will
Heard not her lore, both in subjection now
To sensual appetite, who from beneath
Usurping over sovereign reason claimed
Superior sway: from thus distempered breast,
Adam, estranged in look and altered style,
Speech intermitted thus to Eve renewed.

(IX, 1121–33)

Temperance is not only a characteristic of the true warfaring Puritan, a product of the Platonic rational soul, and the central theme of *The Faerie Queene*, Book II; it is the Aristotelian Golden Mean of human behaviour and, in its most active form, the assertion of the Stoic doctrine of the reason that joins man upward to the divine controlling the passions that join him downward to the brutes. This is where Milton's insistence on free will comes in – an insistence that caused him to break with the Presbyterian section of the Parliamentary party with its stress on predestination and the election of the preordained few (themselves) for salvation. God gave man free will so that he could use his reason to choose between good and evil; for, without this freedom, what possible value could there be in obedience? Again and again Milton stresses this point in *Paradise Lost*. God says of man:

I made him just and right,
Sufficient to have stood, though free to fall.
Such I created all the ethereal powers
And spirits, both them who stood and them who failed;
Freely they stood who stood, and fell who fell.
Not free, what proof could they have given sincere
Of true allegiance, constant faith or love,
Where only what they needs must do, appeared,
Not what they would? What praise could they receive?
What pleasure I from such obedience paid,

When will and reason (reason also is choice)
Useless and vain, of freedom both despoiled,
Made passive both, had served necessity,
Not me. They therefore as to right belonged,
So were created, nor can justly accuse
Their maker, or their making, or their fate,
As if predestination overruled
Their will, disposed by absolute decree
Or high foreknowledge; they themselves decreed
Their own revolt, not I: if I foreknew,
Foreknowledge had no influence on their fault,
Which had no less proved certain unforeknown.

(III, 98–119)

Raphael warns:
Take heed lest passion sway
Thy judgment to do aught, which else free will
Would not admit; . . .
. . . stand fast; to stand or fall
Free in thine own arbitrament it lies.

(VIII, 635–7, 40–1)

Adam says:
But God left free the will, for what obeys
Reason, is free, and reason he made right

(IX, 351–2)

Even Eve tells the serpent in IX, 654: 'our reason is our law'.

Milton tells the story of the Fall in such a way that this individual
freedom of choice is stressed. When Satan seeks to influence Eve's
sleeping mind in the form of a toad (IV, 799–802), he is interrupted: Eve
must be entirely free consciously to choose the way of sin; the choice
must be hers alone. Similarly, God does not allow Gabriel and his patrol
of cherubim to whip Satan back to hell at the end of Book IV, nor Satan
himself to choose vain but glorious resistance; he too must be free to
return and tempt the constancy of mankind.

The general characteristics of Milton's style in *Paradise Lost* are
discussed and illustrated below in the section on style; but one or two of
them pertain particularly to epic, and must be mentioned here. Milton
invokes his Muse four times in *Paradise Lost*, at the beginning of Books
I, III, VII and IX; on each occasion she is a Christian, not a pagan muse,
and he claims that she visits him unsolicited, usually at night, for the
blind Milton composed his verses in bed in the early morning and had
them written down, to be corrected and punctuated later with the help of
one of his nephews. From his Muse Milton hopes to receive an
'answerable style', a style suitable to the grandeur of his chosen subject,

and his style is consciously elevated, as will be seen when it is later analysed in detail. Another epic feature of style is Milton's use of the Homeric simile, a complete word-picture in which a comparison, complete in itself, is made to something or someone in the main narrative. Very often, though not always, these vignettes are taken from Milton's vast Classical learning. Sometimes they cast the incident in the narrative into greater relief by claiming that not even the most celebrated Classical instances of the same thing can compare with what Milton is writing about. Here are some examples from Books IV and IX:

Positive comparison

(*i*) *biblical,*

> so rose the Danite strong
> Herculean Samson from the harlot-lap
> Of philistean Dalilah, and waked
> Shorn of his strength, they destitute and bare
> Of all their virtue
>
> (IX, 1059–63)

(*ii*) *Classical* (quoted below, p. 62)

(*iii*) *non-Classical*, IV, 159–67, 814–19, 980–5; IX, 513–16; 634–43.

Negative comparison

Classical: famous gardens IX, 439–43; famous serpents IX, 503–10; and the most celebrated epic simile in *Paradise Lost*:

> Not that fair field
> Of Enna, where Proserpine gathering flowers
> Her self a fairer flower by gloomy Dis
> Was gathered, which cost Ceres all that pain
> To seek her through the world; nor that sweet grove
> Of Daphne by Orontes, and the inspired
> Castalian spring, might with this Paradise
> Of Eden strive.
>
> (IV, 268–75)

Characters

Satan

Although it is manifestly absurd to suggest that Milton intended Satan to be the hero of *Paradise Lost*, nevertheless the Satan of Books I and II possesses many recognisable characteristics of the epic hero: leadership, initiative, a courage that refuses to accept defeat (I, 105–8), a willingness to undertake the desperate enterprise of escaping from hell and attacking God through his new creation, man. Milton makes no attempt to deny the grandeur of Satan:

> He above the rest
> In shape and gesture proudly eminent
> Stood like a tower; his form had yet not lost
> All her original brightness, nor appeared
> Less than archangel ruined, and the excess
> Of glory obscured.
>
> (I, 589–94)

Milton intended Satan – at least in the early books – to be the representative of the old heroic values which were to be superseded by 'the better fortitude of patience and heroic martyrdom'. Unfortunately for Milton, readers of *Paradise Lost* have recognised the Satanic qualities more readily than the Miltonic. Also, three other factors contributed to the result: in English, the word 'hero' has a meaning of 'central figure', and this Satan certainly is in Books I and II; Milton was strong and fresh creatively when he characterised Satan in these early books; and he never succeeded in producing a rival hero of similar stature but opposed ideals.

Nevertheless, Book IV makes Milton's attitude to Satan very clear; and this is one of the book's main values. Milton – and we – may admire the methods Satan adopts to achieve his aim; but the aim itself is unquestionably evil. Satan is what is called an antinomian: his courage, intelligence and determination are admirable; they are applied, however, in a cause that is not merely unworthy, but hateful. Satan himself is not blind to this; in the lines selected as the dedication of this volume, he turns his back upon good, regret and repentance and chooses the way of evil as offering the best hope of success:

> So farewell hope, and with hope farewell fear,
> Farewell remorse: all good to me is lost;
> Evil be thou my good; by thee at least
> Divided empire with heaven's king I hold
> By thee, and more than half perhaps will raign;
> As man ere long, and this new world shall know.
>
> (IV, 108–13)

From this moment on, when Satan shuts out pity for Adam and Eve, and, filled with envy of their wedded bliss (IV, 505), determines to corrupt their innocence to satisfy his lust for vengeance, Milton sets out to destroy any lingering admiration we may feel for him. Satan takes on, first, the form of a toad and whispers poison in Eve's ear as she lies sleeping (IV, 800); then in Book IX he enters the body of the serpent, 'subtlest beast of all the field' (IX, 86), and in this form carries out his successful temptation of Eve, only to be punished by God (X, 514–17) by being made a serpent for ever. More subtly, Milton changes Satan from a great war-leader into a successful, smooth-tongued and specious politician. As early as Book II, Satan had arranged for Beelzebub to propose (II, 310–416) the mission to earth which he himself would volunteer to undertake, thus confirming his right to leadership. But his arguments to Eve are persuasive in the extreme – they had to be, for Adam and Eve to exchange the bliss of Paradise for disgrace and possible destruction. If I, a serpent, says Satan, have risen a grade, from beast to human (for can I not speak?), you can rise from human to divine. And have I suffered any obvious harm? God will surely not destroy you for improving yourself, for that would be unjust, and He cannot be unjust and still be God; and if He is not God, there is no need to fear or obey Him. If eating the fruit shows you what good is, so much the better; if it reveals the nature of evil to you, how much more prepared you will be to meet it when it comes. The only death there might be is the desirable destruction of your human state in order that your new condition of divinity may begin. By such arguments (IX, 684–702), freely interspersed with blatant flattery, Satan convinces Eve, and Eve later seeks to convince Adam. In addition, Milton shows Satan as using all the artifices of the actor and the orator to bolster up his arguments:

> . . . now more bold
> The tempter, but with show of zeal and love
> To man, and indignation at his wrong,
> New part puts on, and as to passion moved,
> Fluctuates disturbed, yet comely and in act
> Raised, as of some great matter to begin.
> As when of old some orator renowned
> In Athens or free Rome, where eloquence
> Flourished, since mute, to some great cause addressed,
> Stood in himself collected, while each part,
> Motion, each act won audience ere the tongue,
> Sometimes in highth began, as no delay
> Of preface brooking through his zeal of right.
> So standing, moving, or to highth upgrown
> The tempter all impassioned thus began.
>
> (IX, 664–78)

Although this passage contains an epic simile, a classical comparison, in general the later Satan uses – and is described by – much plainer language than the great leader of Books I and II; he has to convince by the content of his arguments, and this makes him much less interesting and attractive poetically.

Adam and Eve

So much of *Paradise Lost* is concerned with the superhuman that the characters of Adam and Eve are of particular interest;* but they too are no ordinary beings, surpassing all their descendants, though each in their different ways:

> Two of far nobler shape erect and tall,
> Godlike erect, with native honour clad
> In naked majesty seemed lords of all,
> And worthy seemed, for in their looks divine
> The image of their glorious maker shone,
> Truth, wisdom, sanctitude severe and pure,
> Severe but in true filial freedom placed;
> Whence true authority in men; though both
> Not equal, as their sex not equal seemed;
> For contemplation he and valour formed,
> For softness she and sweet attractive grace,
> He for God only, she for God in him:
> His fair large front and eye sublime declared
> Absolute rule; . . . the loveliest pair
> That ever since in love's embraces met
> Adam the goodliest man of men since born
> His sons, the fairest of her daughters Eve.
>
> (IV, 288–301; 321–4)

The superiority of Eve over her daughters through time has been obscured by the fact that it is she who sins, and by Milton's obvious bias in favour of the male partner in a marriage. Although he does not go so far as the medieval religious commentators who claimed that, had God intended woman to be man's equal, she would have been taken from his head and not from his side, Milton's prejudice appears unjustifiably strong to the modern reader:

> Thus it shall befall
> Him who to worth in women overtrusting
> Lets her will rule; restraint she will not brook,
> And left to her self, if evil thence ensue,
> She first his weak indulgence will accuse.
>
> (IX, 1182–6)

---

*An added value of the epic similes is that they frequently bring the poem, quite literally, down to earth.

Milton adapts his biblical original to reinforce his point. In Genesis 3:12, Adam shows up as something of a tell-tale: 'the woman . . . gave me of the tree, and I did eat.' In *Paradise Lost* (IX, 820–5) Eve selfishly considers keeping the fruit of the tree of knowledge to herself, partly so that she may become a goddess, but partly also to secure dominion over Adam; she finally decides to share the fruit with him because she does not want to risk being killed, leaving Adam to some other woman!

> Then I shall be no more,
> And Adam wedded to another Eve,
> Shall live with her enjoying, I extinct;
> A death to think.

(IX, 827–30)

Adam's motive in sinning, on the other hand, has its nobler side; he is 'not deceived, but fondly overcome with female charm' (IX, 998–9). He would rather risk death with his beloved Eve than be left alone in Paradise without her if she is destroyed by God in punishment. Satan recognises Adam as the stronger partner and a worthy opponent:

> Her husband, for I view far round, not nigh,
> Whose higher intellectual more I shun,
> And strength, of courage haughty, and of limb
> Heroic built, though of terrestrial mould,
> Foe not informidable.

(IX, 482–6)

Temperance and intemperance

One of the problems concerning Adam and Eve that Milton had to tackle was that of their sexual relationship before the Fall. Many religious commentators would like to believe that sexual relationships did not exist between unfallen man and unfallen woman, partly on the grounds that chastity is the nobler state, but partly also because it supplied a marked and obvious dividing line between unfallen and fallen man. But such a point of view poses the unanswerable question of how the human species was to have been propagated if Adam and Eve had not sinned: Adam, yet sinless, looks forward to the time when 'younger hands' will assist them in their work of keeping the Garden of Eden in order (IX, 246–7). How was this difficulty to be overcome? Of all the solutions proposed – some of them fantastic in the extreme – Milton's seems the most acceptable: he boldly asserts that Adam and Eve enjoyed a full and potentially fruitful sexual relationship before the Fall:

> Nor turned I ween
> Adam from his fair spouse, nor Eve the rites

Mysterious of connubial love refused:
Whatever hypocrites austerely talk
Of purity and place and innocence,
Defaming as impure what God declares
Pure, and commands to some, leaves free to all.
Our maker bids increase, who bids abstain
But our destroyer, foe to God and man?

(IV, 741-9)

Straightway Milton passes on to a hymn in praise of wedded love, a love
which seems to arouse the anger and envy of Satan more than anything
else:

Hail wedded love, mysterious law, true source
Of human offspring, sole propriety
In Paradise of all things common else.
By thee adulterous lust was driven from men
Among the bestial herds to range, by thee
Founded in reason, loyal, just, and pure,
Relations dear, and all the charities
Of father, son, and brother first were known.
Far be it, that I should write thee sin or blame,
Or think thee unbefitting holiest place,
Perpetual fountain of domestic sweets,
Whose bed is undefiled and chaste pronounced.

(IV, 750-1)

These lines contain the core of Milton's thinking on the subject: what is
sinful is not physical lovemaking, but mindless lust. The reason that
distinguishes mankind from the beasts must always be in control; love
must indeed be founded in reason, loyal, just, and pure'. The archangel
Raphael, leaving the Garden at the end of Book VIII, gives Adam this
warning at parting:

In loving thou dost well, in passion not,
Wherein true love consists not; love refines
The thoughts, and heart enlarges, hath his seat
In reason, and is judicious, is the scale
By which to heavenly love thou mayst ascend,
Not sunk in carnal pleasure, for which cause
Among the beasts no mate for thee was found.

(VIII, 588-94)

It is the doctrine of temperance in its most obvious manifestation: the
passions that link us to the beasts must always be controlled by the
reason that joins us to God and which, left free, gives us the power to

choose between good and evil and makes our obedience worth while. To Milton, man falls through intemperance: Samson in *Samson Agonistes* loses his strength not because his hair is shorn, but because he allows his passion for Delilah to overcome his reason; and Adam and Eve fall, not because they eat a forbidden apple, but because its aphrodisiac qualities make them lust for each other and forget their reasonable love:

> They swim in mirth, and fancy that they feel
> Divinity within them breeding wings
> Wherewith to scorn the earth: but that false fruit
> Far other operation first displayed,
> Carnal desire inflaming, he on Eve
> Began to cast lascivious eyes, she him
> As wantonly repaid; in lust they burn ...
> So said he, and forbore not glance or toy
> Of amorous intent, well understood
> Of Eve, whose eye darted contagious fire.
> Her hand he seized, and to a shady bank,
> Thick overhead with verdant roof embowered
> He led her nothing loth; flowers were the couch,
> Pansies, and violets, and asphodel,
> And hyacinth, earth's freshest softest lap.
> There they their fill of love and love's disport
> Took largely, of their mutual guilt the seal,
> The solace of their sin, till dewy sleep
> Oppressed them, wearied with their amorous play.
>
> (IX, 1009–15 and 1034–45)

The Garden of Eden

Although man's fall through intemperance is the focal point of *Paradise Lost*, and makes Book IX the central book of the poem, the background against which it takes place is significant. From the lofty empyrean and the burning depths of hell and the limitless profound of the realm of Chaos and old Night, we come to rest with considerable relief in Book IV in a garden on our own planet. Strictly, Eden is the area of land and Paradise is the garden on top of a wooded hill set in the eastern part of it; but the two names are used loosely, and the thief on Calvary to whom Christ promised he would that night be with Him in Paradise knew that he would find himself in Heaven, not Eden.

Unfortunately, Milton's descriptions of the garden leave much to be desired as nature poetry. There is no reason to doubt that Milton loved nature, but he relied for his descriptions of the supreme beauty of Eden less on what Dante calls 'the memory of the eye' (his blindness should not be forgotten) than on comparing Paradise to the most celebrated gardens of the Classics:

> Spot more delicious than those gardens feigned
> Or of revived Adonis, or renowned
> Alcinous, host of old Laertes' son,
> Or that, not mystic, where the sapient king
> Held dalliance with his fair Egyptian spouse.
> (IX, 439–43; see also the Enna simile quoted on p. 55)

Alternatively, Milton paraphrases the early chapters on Genesis (see notes to IV, 195; 209; 223), and his reliance on these two literary sources for his natural descriptions, added to his use of a specialised poetic diction (see pp. 67–8) justifies the comment that he is a poet who looked at nature through the spectacles of books. His description of the flowers in Eden echoes the list of flowers – itself conventional – with which he had strewn the grave of Lycidas in 1637:

> Bring the rathe Primrose that forsaken dies.
> The tufted Crow-toe, and pale Gessamine,
> The white Pink, and the Pansie freakt with jeat,
> The glowing Violet.
> The Musk-rose, and the well attir'd Woodbine.
> With Cowslips wan that hang the pensive hed,
> And every flower that sad embroidery wears:
> Bid Amaranthus all his beauty shed,
> And Daffadillies fill their cups with tears,
> To strew the Laureat Herse where Lycid lies.
> (*Lycidas*, 142–51)

> It was a place
> Chosen by the sovereign planter, when he framed
> All things to man's delightful use; the roof
> Of thickest covert was inwoven shade
> Laurel and myrtle, and what higher grew
> Of firm and fragrant leaf; on either side
> Acanthus, and each odorous bushy shrub
> Fenced up the verdant wall; each beauteous flower,
> Iris all hues, roses, and jessamine
> Reared high their flourished heads between, and wrought
> Mosaic; underfoot the violet,
> Crocus, and hyacinth with rich inlay
> Broidered the ground, more coloured than with stone
> Of costliest emblem.
> (IV, 690–703)

Milton's natural descriptions do not lack beauty: but it is a beauty of art rather than nature, of sound rather than of sight:

> Now came still evening on, and twilight grey
> Had in her sober livery all things clad;
> Silence accompanied, for beast and bird,
> They to their grassy couch, these to their nests
> Were slunk, all but the wakeful nightingale;
> She all night long her amorous descant sung.
>
> (IV, 598–603)

Style

Milton would certainly not have agreed with John Keats's (1795–1821) comment that if poetry comes not as naturally as leaves to a tree it had better not come at all (*Letter* 51). He was a supremely conscious artist, and sought to elevate his style to a height where it would match the grandeur of his epic subject. A close and detailed analysis of this style is therefore essential, difficult though it may sometimes be and often consisting of rather dull lists of accumulated examples. To Milton, the style was as important as the content it carried; his prefatory note to the poem is about his verse medium, 'English heroic verse without rhyme'; in *Paradise Lost* this is divided into long sentence-paragraphs with complicated syntax – the first full stop comes at the end of the sixteenth line! His blindness made Milton hypersensitive to the value of sound in poetry, and his verse becomes richer if read aloud in accordance with the indications given by his original spelling and punctuation; for example, a personal pronoun receives additional stress by being moved to the beginning of a sentence and by doubling its vowel – 'Mee miserable' in IV, 73; while the presence of an apostrophe indicates that the root vowel in a weak past tense or participle was intended to be pronounced long:

> So gloz'd the Tempter, and his Proem tun'd;
> (IX, 549 in Oxford Standard *Milton*, 1950)

When dealing with such a conscious artist, it is essential for a student to give due weight to the elements in his style.

Latin vocabulary

Milton was a distinguished Latin scholar, and Books IV and IX contain many words translated directly from the Latin or used with their Latin rather than their more usual English signification. Here are some of the most striking:

Book IV   186 (and elsewhere) *secure* = over-confident (*securus*)

	239	*pendant* = hanging
	300 (and elsewhere)	*front* = forehead *(frons)*
	594	*diurnal* = in its daily movement
	688	*divide the night into watches (dividere noctem)*
	869	*port* = bearing
	938 (and elsewhere)	*fame* = rumour *(fama)*
	1000	*pendulous* = hanging
Book IX:	104	*officious* = fulfilling their office *(officiosus)*
	142	*name* = family *(nama)*
	170 and 1094	*obnoxious* = exposed to *(obnoxius)*
	186	*nocent* = hateful
	503	*redundant* = overflowing
	748	*elocution* = power of speech
	837	*sciential* = having knowledge
	1117	*cincture* = encircling girdle

Inversions

Another Latin characteristic much favoured by Milton is the inversion of the normal word order of an adjective followed by the substantive it qualifies; these inversions are so marked a feature of Milton's style that they were imitated by Keats in *Hyperion*, his unfinished attempt at writing a Miltonic epic. Here is a selection from Books IV and IX:

Book IV:	118 *distempers foul*	128 *gestures fierce*	
	133 *enclosure green*	144 *prospect large*	
	347 *serpent sly*	350 *proof unheeded*	
	571 *passions foul*	795 *errand bad*	
	840 *doom obscure*	916 *anger infinite*	
Book IX:	39 *office mean*	141 *servitude inglorious*	
	227 *associate sole*	461 *rapine sweet*	
	495 *inmate bad*	510 *tract oblique*	
	548 *angels numberless*	566 *attention due*	
	732 *goddess humane*	771 *author unsuspect*	
	864 *danger tasted*	867 *serpent wise*	
	890 *horror chill*	927 *God omnipotent*	
	938 *creator wise*	962 *example high*	

Adjectives on each side

A peculiarly Miltonic extension of the inversion is the enriching of his descriptions by balancing an adjective on each side of the noun; again a selection of examples from both books is given:

Book IV: 361 *heavenly spirits bright*
486 *individual solace dear*
493 *conjugal attraction unreproved*
503 *jealous leer malign*
647 *grateful evening mild*
870 *failed splendour wan*

Book IX: 5   *venial discourse unblamed*
45 *my intended wing depressed*
228 *all living creatures dear*
409 *hellish rancour imminent*
529 *serpent tongue organic*
577 *fairest colours mixed*
983 *faithful love unequalled*
1003 *mortal sin original*
1047 *exhilarating vapour bland*

Sound values

Milton shows his awareness of sound-values in a number of ways. Here are three of them:

1. By the use of words derived from sources different from the normal and which, while etymologically justifiable, show the reader more precisely than the usual form exactly how Milton intended the word to be pronounced: IV, 691, 'sovran', from Italian *sovrano*, as opposed to 'sovereign', a word of a variable number of syllables derived from Old French *souverain*; IX, 675; 677, 'highth' from Old English *híehtho*, in preference to 'height'.

2. Collections of resounding proper names, which Milton rolls out in those epic comparisons of Eden to famous beauty-spots in the classics (IV, 268–75, quoted on p. 55), or in the geographical summary of Satan's nocturnal wanderings following his expulsion from Eden by Gabriel and his patrol of cherubim:

Sea he had searched and land
From Eden over Pontus, and the pool
Maeotis, up beyond the river Ob;
Downward as far antarctic; and in length
West from Orontes to the ocean barred
At Darien, thence to the land where flows
Ganges and Indus: thus the orb he roamed
With narrow search.

(IX, 76–83)

3. In two magnificent lines Milton sums up, by the use of sound alone, the contrast between the grandeur of Satan the invader of Eden and the snivelling triviality of the clergy who in Milton's own times schemed their way into preferment:

> So clomb this first grand thief into God's fold:
> So since into his church lewd hirelings climb.
> (IV, 192–3)

Notice in the first of these lines the rounded vowels *a* and *o*, and the lengthening combinations of consonants '-ld' and '-nd'; best of all the creation of a strong past tense 'clomb' in place of the normal weak past 'climbed', mutating the vowel instead of merely adding '-ed'. It is now impossible to read this line without giving it a full, rounded, sonorous quality. The next line, a contrast in sound much as in content, is full of narrow vowels and sibilants – mean 'i's and hissing 's's. Nowhere else in so short a space does Milton show greater control of sound-values.

Word dualism

Milton indulges in a number of varieties of verbal gymnastics in *Paradise Lost*. The most striking is dualism of derivation. Sometimes an English word can justifiably be derived from two different roots in two different languages: an example is the phrase, occurring twice (IV, 642 and 651), 'charm of earliest birds'; 'charm' can be traced to Latin *carmen*, song, or to Middle English *cherme* from Old English *cyrm*, noise of birds. Milton specifically calls attention to this device in a passage in Book IX:

> Eve, now I see thou art exact of taste,
> And elegant, of sapience no small part,
> Since to each meaning savour we apply.
> (IX, 1017–19)

Here both 'sapience', discernment, and 'savour', tastiness, derive ultimately from the same Latin verb, *sapere*.

More often, Milton plays upon the possible double meaning of a word: some are obvious (IX, 358); some far-fetched (IX, 1067, where the word 'evil' is derived from the name 'Eve'); some require an explanation or specialised knowledge (IV, 354, where 'scale' has its normal meaning but also refers to the zodiacal sign of Libra, the Scales). Here is a short list of these quibbles:

Book IV: 181 'bound', jump; 'bound', boundary, restraint
          286 'saw undelighted all delight'
          354 'ascending scale' (see above)

Book IX: 200 'prime', first; 'prime', choicest
          358 'mind', care for; 'mind', take notice of
          613 'spirited', energetic; 'spirited', possessed by a spirit
          648 'fruitless', useless; 'fruit' (normal meaning)
          1067 'Eve . . . evil' (see above)

Of particular interest is one type of apparently straightforward repetition – epanalepsis – where the recurrence of a word or phrase serves to bind the sentence more closely together: this is particularly important in Milton's long sentence-paragraphs, and to some extent takes over the function normally exercised by syntax. Two examples must suffice here in view of the length, but references to others are given below:

Happy, but for so happy ill secured
Long to continue, and this high seat your heaven
Ill fenced for heaven to keep out such a foe
As now is entered; yet no purposed foe
To you whom I could pity thus forlorn
Though I unpitied.
                    (IV, 370–5)

Sweet is the breath of morn, her rising sweet,
With charm of earliest birds; pleasant the sun
When first on this delightful land he spreads
His orient beams, on herb, tree, fruit, and flower,
Glistering with dew; fragrant the fertile earth
After soft showers; and sweet the coming on
Of grateful evening mild, then silent night
With this her solemn bird and this fair moon,
And these the gems of heaven, her starry train:
But neither breath of morn when she ascends
With charm of earliest birds, nor rising sun
On this delightful land, nor herb, fruit, flower
Glistering with dew, nor fragrance after showers,
Nor grateful evening mild, nor silent night
With this her solemn bird, nor walk by moon,
Or glittering starlight without thee is sweet.
                    (IV, 641–56)
Other References: IV, 7–8; 950–2; IX, 176–8; 475–9; 938–54.

Poetic diction

The charge that Milton's natural descriptions are artificial depends partly upon the so-called poetic diction he employs – a language divorced from the everyday speech of man and using instead polysyllabic Latinisms, inversions and circumlocutions. Favourite examples include the 'gentle gales' of IV, 156, instead of 'breezes', the 'grassy herb' and 'trodden herb'for 'grass' in IX, 186 and 572; and best of all the 'lithe proboscis' of the elephant in IV, 347. Admittedly, these usages do strike the modern reader as unnatural; but the real culprits are Milton's eighteenth-century imitators, who thought they had only to call the sun 'the grand luminary' or fish 'the finny tribe' or a spade 'metallic blade wedded to ligneus rod' to be writing great poetry. This problem of poetic diction is really no problem at all: a poet can use Teutonic monosyllables and write great poetry; equally, he can use Latin polysyllables and write great poetry; or he can write bad poetry in either. What matters is the strength of the creative genius he applies to the medium he chooses; and this strength Milton had and his later imitators lacked. Milton asked his celestial patroness for a style to match the high seriousness of his universal subject of the fall of man. The foregoing study of his style should have clearly established that he certainly received it.

Part 4

Hints for study

Answering questions on the text

Three main types of written answer can be demanded: (*1*) The one written in your own time and with full reference to texts, works of criticism and biography, and all other aids; (*2*) the one written for an examination, in a limited time, but with reference to the text – but only the text – permitted; (*3*) the one written under strict examination conditions with a time limit and no external aids allowed. The reason for differentiating between (*2*) and (*3*) is the increasing tendency to reward sound critical judgement rather than the gift of a good memory.

Answer: type (1)

There is a mistaken idea in many educational institutions of what the aim of a literary examination is: it is *not* to give the candidates the opportunity to regurgitate all the information they have amassed about the writer and his works whose name appears in the question. Remember:

(*i*) Select only that part of your knowledge or the material available to you which is strictly relevant to the question asked.

(*ii*) Read the actual text on the syllabus as often as you can and try to tell the examiner about its effect on you personally.

(*iii*) Although works of criticism by highly qualified specialists in the subject are valuable, they should be read to provoke thought and stimulate ideas only *after* you have read the text thoroughly and thought about it carefully.

(*iv*) Similarly with quotations: they should illustrate your point of view and strengthen your argument; but they must not become an end in themselves. An examiner will not relish – or reward – an essay that is three parts Milton and only one part candidate; he wants to know the candidate's views, which should be judiciously supported by quotations from and references to Milton's text.

Answers: types (2) and (3)

(*i*) Know the text that has been set on the syllabus thoroughly before you go into the examination. Although a final read-through of the text is advisable, do not read works of criticism, sets of notes, or prepared answers just before the examination, for two reasons: what you have just read will be uppermost in your mind, and will unbalance the proportionate importance of your material; secondly, if a question similar but not identical to one you have just been revising appears in the paper, you will tend to force the question to fit your prepared answer instead of writing an answer matched to the actual question. In both these cases, you will lose marks for irrelevance, the most common cause of failure in literary examinations.

(*ii*) After reading the question carefully, jot down the topics of major interest which it raises. These are going to become your paragraph headings; there should be at least three of them so that, with an introduction and a conclusion, you will have the optimum number of five paragraphs of average length – more if shorter, though fewer are rarely justified. Written answers should always conclude, never just stop; and each paragraph should deal with a different aspect of the question, though if you can run one paragraph smoothly into the next by arranging your subject-matter logically, so much the better.

(*iii*) Under your paragraph headings, jot down supporting references from the text; in (*2*) you will be able to note the line numbers from your text, but in (*3*) you will have to remember some word or phrase that will recall the required quotation or reference to mind when the time comes. At first, you will have to read the text through once for each heading, looking for supporting material; but, as you gain experience, you will be able to allocate your references to the different paragraphs by reading through the text once only.

(*iv*) Take each paragraph-sheet separately and re-arrange the subsidiary points into a coherent and progressive argument, moving your line-references out of strict chronological order to follow the ideas to which they belong.

(*v*) From your new plan, write out your answer, adding a brief introductory paragraph and a conclusion. In (*2*), your line-references will now become quotations, in (*3*) they should be short quotations if you know them by heart, or references to show that you know the text. Remember that, if you do this, no examiner will penalise you, however much he may personally disagree with your interpretation. After all, what he is looking for is critical judgement and originality and independence of mind, not just the ability to sop up huge quantities of second- or third-hand material like a sponge, to be squeezed whenever the opportunity presents itself.

Types of question set on 'Paradise Lost', Books IV and IX

Let us apply these principles to *Paradise Lost*, Books IV and IX. The first essay in category (*1*) would be 'what are the main themes treated by Milton in *Paradise Lost*, Books IV and IX?' The answer to this is contained in the Detailed Summaries and, in greater detail, in the Commentary. The purpose of the question is to make the student familiarise himself thoroughly with the text. Next we proceed to subjects which can be covered by a close examination of the text alone, an intelligent analysis of the meaning, and a coherent presentation of the content in your own words; for instance, 'Summarise Satan's reasons for continued resistance advanced in his address to the sun in Book IV', or, even better, 'Summarise the arguments advanced by Satan in his successful temptation of Eve in Book IX'. Next, some topics which require background knowledge – say on epic poetry – and on which some instruction has been given; for instance, 'What criticisms has Milton to offer on earlier epic, and what does he propose to put in its place?' (The material for this answer will be found on pp. 50–5). Next comes the type of question which necessitates the painstaking collection of material from the text – a test of your powers of application – its re-arrangement and presentation as a unified and coherent answer; for instance, 'Illustrate the principal characteristics of Milton's style in *Paradise Lost*, Books IV and IX' (see pp. 63–8). Finally, there is the question which demands a considerable amount of thought and originality from the individual student, plus a sound knowledge of the text on which he can draw to support his point of view by quotation and reference; for instance, 'Comment on the change in the relationship of Adam and Eve in *Paradise Lost*, Books IV and IX' (see pp. 58–9).

Specimen question

It would be valuable to take at least one question not answered in the course of this study and to show how the question might be tackled – a practical example of how to write a Milton essay.

Show how Milton uses biblical material in *Paradise Lost*, Books IV and IX

To Milton and his contemporaries, the Bible was regarded as divinely inspired Holy Writ, and its wording was not lightly to be tampered with. The first thing to notice is that Milton uses creative freedom in those parts of the narrative not covered by the Bible; but where the Bible story is followed, Milton's wording is so close as to be almost a poetic paraphrase.

There are three main areas covered by both Milton and the Bible: the description of the Garden of Eden; the temptation and fall of mankind; and the relationship of husband and wife. The first two themes are based on Genesis, and make an interesting contrast. Because the description of Eden in Genesis 2 is detailed, Milton follows it closely. Let us look at some examples:

And the Lord God planted a garden eastward in Eden; and there he put the man whom he had formed.

And out of the ground made the Lord God to grow every tree that is pleasant to the sight, and good for food; the tree of life also in the midst of the garden, and the tree of knowledge of good and evil.

And a river went out of Eden to water the garden; and from thence it was parted, and became into four heads.

(Genesis 2:8–10)

Now let us turn to Milton's description of the Garden of Eden in *Paradise Lost*, Book IV:

For blissful Paradise
Of God the garden was, by him in the east
Of Eden planted.   (IV, 208–10)

The tree of life
The middle tree and highest there that grew.   (IV, 194–5)

In this pleasant soil
His far more pleasant garden God ordained;
Out of the fertile ground he caused to grow
All trees of noblest kind for sight, smell, taste;
And all amid them stood the tree of life.   (IV, 214–18)

Southward through Eden went a river large –
And now divided into four main streams.   (IV, 223; 233)

The whole of Milton's description of Paradise (IV, 131–268) is full of verbal reminiscences of Genesis 2 and 3; for Milton was quite prepared to rely on written authority – and so impeccable a written authority – for his descriptions of nature. And he was prepared to rely on St Paul's sentiments regarding the subjection of a wife to a husband – because they coincided so exactly with his own!

and the head of the woman is the man (1 Corinthians 11:3).

To whom thus Eve replied. O thou for whom
And from whom I was formed flesh of thy flesh,
And without whom am to no end, my guide
And head.   (*Paradise Lost* IV, 440–3)

Let us go back to the second Miltonic theme based on the early chapters of Genesis, the temptation and fall of man. Here Milton adapts the scriptural text to suit his own ideas. There is actually in the Bible no specific identification of the tempting serpent with Satan the arch-fiend: most Englishmen have absorbed this conviction in childhood – from Milton! There is no discussion of wedded love or of sex before the Fall in Genesis, and the sin of Adam and Eve is one of disobedience rather than intemperance. The actual arguments used by the serpent in his temptation of Eve are not given in Genesis 3 as they are in *Paradise Lost*, IX. There are no rational souls or souls irrational through lust and anger, no free will or free choice. With these last Milton adds to the story without contradicting Genesis: for Satan to make an unsuccessful attempt on Eve in Book IV adds to the interest of his successful effort in Book IX, when her will is entirely free to make its own choice. Perhaps the most significant adaptation – small but significant – is the change of emphasis in the admission of responsibility. In Genesis 3:12, Adam says 'The woman . . . gave me of the tree, and I did eat'. In *Paradise Lost*, a much nobler Adam, 'not deceived, but fondly overcome with female charm' (IX, 999), declares that he would rather die with Eve than live without her.

> With thee
> Certain my resolution is to die;
> How can I live without thee, how forgo
> Thy sweet converse and love so dearly joined,
> To live again in these wild woods forlorn?
> Should God create another Eve, and I
> Another rib afford, yet loss of thee
> Would never from my heart; no no, I feel
> The link of nature draw me: flesh of flesh,
> Bone of my bone thou art, and from thy state
> Mine never shall be parted, bliss or woe.
>
> (IX, 906–16)

Apart from his main themes, Milton uses the Bible for some of his incidental references and epic comparisons. The reference to Asmodeus and the stinking fish (IV, 168–71) is taken from the Apocryphal Book of Tobit 6:8, Solomon as a garden-lover (IX, 442) from the Song of Solomon 6:2, and the last epic simile in Book IX (1059–61) compares the shame of Adam to the shame of Samson. Sometimes, too, Milton supplements the Bible from other sources: Gabriel as a warrior angel from early Jewish traditions; an alternative site for Paradise from the seventeenth-century geographer Heylyn; and the details of the fig-leaves with which Adam and Eve cover their nakedness from Pliny's *Natural History* by way of Gerard's *Herball* (1597).

To sum up: Milton uses his biblical source for three of his main themes in *Paradise Lost*, IV and IX – the description of Eden, the temptation and fall of man, and the relationship of husband and wife; and also for a number of incidental references. Where the Bible is detailed or specific, Milton tends to follow it closely. But where he is given an opportunity to expand the Bible narrative from his own vast store of knowledge he does not hesitate to do so. And where he wishes to stress his own ideas – and even prejudices in the case of husbandly dominion – he does not hesitate to adapt his scriptural original.

Part 5

Suggestions for further reading

The text

SUMNER, C. R. (ed.): *Milton's Prose Works*, 5 vols., Bohn, London, 1848–53. Easier to handle than the Columbia edition.

Milton's Poetical Works in Oxford Standard Authors, Oxford University Press, London, 1904, revised 1969. Retains the original spelling: important for Milton.

VERITY, A. W.: *Milton, 'Paradise Lost'*, 2 vols., Cambridge University Press, Cambridge, 1936. Good notes in vol. II.

CAREY, J. AND FOWLER, A. (eds.): *Milton* in Longmans Annotated English Poets, Longman, London, 1966. Full and erudite annotations and cross-references.

Milton's Complete Works in Columbia edition, 18 vols., University of Columbia Press, New York, 1931–8. Definitive edition of text.

Biographies and criticism

DIEKHOFF, J. S.: *Milton on Himself,* Cohen & West, London, 1966. Excellent collection of significant quotations from Milton's work.

HANDFORD, J. H.: *A Milton Handbook*, F. S. Crofts & Co., New York, 1946. Essential to any thoughtful student of *Paradise Lost.*

PETER, J.: *A Critique of 'Paradise Lost'*, Longmans, London, 1961. Good on the Fall.

TILLYARD, E. M. W.: *The Miltonic Setting*, Chatto & Windus, London, 1957. Essays on essential Miltonic topics.

WALDOCK, A. J. A.: *'Paradise Lost' and its Critics*, Cambridge University Press, Cambridge, 1947. Miltonic critical theories.

Background

ABERCROMBIE, L.: *The Epic,* 'The art and craft of letters', Secker, London, 1914. Characteristics and history of epic poetry.

BOWRA, C. M.: *From Virgil to Milton*, Macmillan, London, 1945. Excellent on the evolution of epic.

NICOLSON, M. H.: *The Breaking of the Circle*, Oxford University Press, London, 1960. Excellent on the cosmological background of the seventeenth century.

The author of these notes

RICHARD JAMES BECK was educated at Jesus College, Oxford, and St Andrews University. His undergraduate career was interrupted by service as a bomber pilot; he was shot down and during his three and a half years as a prisoner-of-war in Germany he taught *Paradise Lost* in the so-called Barbed Wire University. He was a lecturer in the University of St Andrews before being appointed Professor of English in the University of Malta. In 1975 he was created an Officer of the British Empire 'for services to education in Malta'. He died unexpectedly in 1979.

His publications include an edition of Chaucer's *Preamble and Tale of the Wife of Bath* (1964); a critical introduction to Shakespeare's *Henry IV* in Arnold's *Studies in Literature*, (1965); and a volume in this series of York Notes on *Paradise Lost*, Books I and II. He also wrote articles for various learned journals, largely on Chaucer and Milton.

The first 100 titles

CHINUA ACHEBE	*Arrow of God* *Things Fall Apart*
JANE AUSTEN	*Northanger Abbey* *Pride and Prejudice* *Sense and Sensibility*
ROBERT BOLT	*A Man For All Seasons*
CHARLOTTE BRONTË	*Jane Eyre*
EMILY BRONTË	*Wuthering Heights*
ALBERT CAMUS	*L'Etranger (The Outsider)*
GEOFFREY CHAUCER	*Prologue to the Canterbury Tales* *The Franklin's Tale* *The Knight's Tale* *The Nun's Priest's Tale* *The Pardoner's Tale*
SIR ARTHUR CONAN DOYLE	*The Hound of the Baskervilles*
JOSEPH CONRAD	*Nostromo*
DANIEL DEFOE	*Robinson Crusoe*
CHARLES DICKENS	*David Copperfield* *Great Expectations*
GEORGE ELIOT	*Adam Bede* *Silas Marner* *The Mill on the Floss*
T. S. ELIOT	*The Waste Land*
WILLIAM FAULKNER	*As I Lay Dying*
F. SCOTT FITZGERALD	*The Great Gatsby*
E. M. FORSTER	*A Passage to India*
ATHOL FUGARD	*Selected Plays*
MRS GASKELL	*North and South*
WILLIAM GOLDING	*Lord of the Flies*

OLIVER GOLDSMITH	*The Vicar of Wakefield*
THOMAS HARDY	*Jude the Obscure*
	Tess of the D'Urbervilles
	The Mayor of Casterbridge
	The Return of the Native
	The Trumpet Major
L. P. HARTLEY	*The Go-Between*
ERNEST HEMINGWAY	*For Whom the Bell Tolls*
	The Old Man and the Sea
ANTHONY HOPE	*The Prisoner of Zenda*
RICHARD HUGHES	*A High Wind in Jamaica*
THOMAS HUGHES	*Tom Brown's Schooldays*
HENRIK IBSEN	*A Doll's House*
HENRY JAMES	*The Turn of the Screw*
BEN JONSON	*The Alchemist*
	Volpone
D. H. LAWRENCE	*Sons and Lovers*
	The Rainbow
HARPER LEE	*To Kill a Mocking-Bird*
SOMERSET MAUGHAM	*Selected Short Stories*
HERMAN MELVILLE	*Billy Budd*
	Moby Dick
ARTHUR MILLER	*Death of a Salesman*
	The Crucible
JOHN MILTON	*Paradise Lost I & II*
SEAN O'CASEY	*Juno and the Paycock*
GEORGE ORWELL	*Animal Farm*
	Nineteen Eighty-four
JOHN OSBORNE	*Look Back in Anger*
HAROLD PINTER	*The Birthday Party*
J. D. SALINGER	*The Catcher in the Rye*
SIR WALTER SCOTT	*Ivanhoe*
	Quentin Durward

WILLIAM SHAKESPEARE	*A Midsummer Night's Dream*
	Antony and Cleopatra
	Coriolanus
	Cymbeline
	Hamlet
	Henry IV Part I
	Henry V
	Julius Caesar
	King Lear
	Macbeth
	Measure for Measure
	Othello
	Richard II
	Romeo and Juliet
	The Merchant of Venice
	The Tempest
	The Winter's Tale
	Troilus and Cressida
	Twelfth Night
GEORGE BERNARD SHAW	*Androcles and the Lion*
	Arms and the Man
	Caesar and Cleopatra
	Pygmalion
RICHARD BRINSLEY SHERIDAN	*The School for Scandal*
JOHN STEINBECK	*Of Mice and Men*
	The Grapes of Wrath
	The Pearl
ROBERT LOUIS STEVENSON	*Kidnapped*
	Treasure Island
JONATHAN SWIFT	*Gulliver's Travels*
W. M. THACKERAY	*Vanity Fair*
MARK TWAIN	*Huckleberry Finn*
	Tom Sawyer
VOLTAIRE	*Candide*
H. G. WELLS	*The History of Mr Polly*
	The Invisible Man
	The War of the Worlds
OSCAR WILDE	*The Importance of Being Earnest*